# NUT**SHELLS**

## Land Law

# YOU'VE GOT IT
# CRACKED

# NUT**SHELLS**

# Land Law

by
**MICHAEL HALEY**
Solicitor,
Professor of Law,
Keele University

**SWEET & MAXWELL**

THOMSON REUTERS

First Edition – 1987
Second Edition – 1991
Third Edition – 1994
Reprinted – 1997
Fourth Edition – 1997
Fifth Edition – 2000
Reprinted – 2001
Reprinted – 2002
Reprinted – 2003
Sixth Edition – 2004
Seventh Edition – 2007

Published in 2010 by Thomson Reulers (Legal) Limited
(Registered in England & Wales, Company No 1679046.
Registered Office and address for service:
100 Avenue Road, London NW3 3PF)
trading as Sweet & Maxwell

*For further information on our products and services, visit
www.sweetandmaxwell.co.uk*

Typeset by LBJ Typesetting Ltd
Printed in Great Britain by Ashford Colour Press Ltd, Gosport, Hants

*No natural forests were destroyed to make this product;
only farmed timber was used and re-planted*

A CIP catalogue record for this book is available from the British Library.

ISBN: 9780414041769

Thomson Reuters and the Thomson Reuters logo are trademarks of Thomson Reuters.
Sweet & Maxwell ® is a registered trademark of Thomson Reuters (Legal) Limited.

# Contents

# Using this Book

Welcome to our new took **NUTSHELLS** revision series. We have revamped and improved the existing design and layout and added new features, according to student feedback.

**NEW DETAILED TABLE OF CONTENTS**
for easy navigation.

## Contents

**REDESIGNED TABLES OF CASES
AND LEGISLATION** for easy reference.

## Table of Cases

**NEW CHAPTER INTRODUCTIONS** to outline the key concepts covered and condense complex and important information.

**INTRODUCTION**

English law makes a primary distinction between (realty and personality). Although the peculiar Engli an exception, this distinction corresponds in the m in civil law systems between immovable and mova significance of this distinction is that real propert the ability to bind future purchasers of the land v as a licence) do not. The language employed, and, at first, apt to confuse.

Figure 1

**DEFINITION CHECKPOINTS, EXPLANATION OF KEY CASES AND LEGISLATION HIGHLIGHTERS** to highlight important information.

...nsequently, it is more ...ssion (seisin) in determining titl

**DEFINITION CHECKPOINT**

In the physical sense, land includes not only but also all buildings on the land, any fixture and minerals and any incorporeal rights such of the **Law of Property Act 1925**. At common la is said to extend up to the sky and down to th *est solum, eius est usque ad coelum et ad ir*

...nace

...s remedy can be orderec that the patent is inextricably e.

**KEY CASE**

**KIRIN-AMGEN INC V TRANSKARYOTIC THEARA**
In *Kirin-Amgen Inc v Transkaryotic Thec* cells carrying small amounts of patented pr delivery up.

(c) Court order for a party to reveal relev Procedure Rules (rule 31) such an orde for example, the name and address of along with the traditional discr Norwich Pharmacal order (af ...ators as the

...to a reason...

...ions. Alongside the add ...ne Patent Rules.

**LEGISLATION HIGHLIGHTER**

The Patent Rules 2007 (No. 3291), Pa and Patents (Compulsory Licensin Certificate) Regulations 2007 (No. 32 patent system.

...TAINING A PATENT

## DIAGRAMS, FLOWCHARTS AND OTHER
DIAGRAMMATIC REPRESENTATION to clarify
and condense complex and important
information and breakup the text.

...ligation imposed on a third p...
...mes vested), to act for the benefit of anot...
... The equitable interest in property thereby bec...
...t form the nominal legal ownership vested in the truste...

**The Trust Relationship**

Settlor ———— Legal Title ————→ Trustee

Equitable Title                    Rights   D...

Beneficiary

...the language employed, however...
...confuse.

Property

Real (immovables)
Freehold land

Personal (movables)

Corporeal
...reditaments

Incorporeal
Hereditaments

Chattels
Real

Chattels
Personal

Choses in
Action

Choses in
Possessio...

...ble Right to Redeem
...he right of a mortgagor (borrower) to redeem the m...
...f capital, interest and costs) even after the l...
...tion has passed (see Ch.10). Equi...
...ot subject to cloes ...

**...SS OF PROPERTY**

...the term applied ...

## END OF CHAPTER REVISION
## CHECKLISTS outlining what you
should now know and understand.

...1977 than that wri...
...ovision fell squarely within art. ...
...of the discriminatory nature of the pr...
legitimate justification for this differen...
provision so as to give equal rights to all ...

### Revision Checklist

You should now know and understand:

- the various classifications of proper...
- what is meant by the term "land";
- how to distinguish a fixture fro...
- the possible impact of hu...

## END OF CHAPTER QUESTION AND
## ANSWER SECTION with advice on
relating knowledge to examination
performance, how to approach
the question, how to structure the
answer, the pitfalls (and how to
avoid them!) and how to get the
best marks.

### QUESTION AND ANSWER

#### Question

James enters into a contract to purchase
The building is fitted throughout with expe
paneling and exotic wall tapestries. The
collection of stuffed creatures, some of
wall cabinets. The grounds are styled to
feature free-standing traditional huts ...
wishes to remove the above named ...
Advise Kirk.

**HANDY HINTS**
– revision and examination tips and advice
relating to the subject features at the end
of the book.

**HANDY HINTS**

The golden rule for most law examinati
*all* of the question (i.e. all its constituer
(i.e. do not digress, keep your answer re
revision, practice and planning all have

Some issues may require discus
questions may involve breach of confi
also require consideration of passi

̴ation

**NEW COLOUR CODING** throughout to
help distinguish cases and legislation
from the narrative. At the first mention,
cases are highlighted in colour and
italicised and legislation is highlighted
in colour and emboldened.

̴es (Chattels Real)

Historically, leases were treated as pers
a personal action could be taken for disp
was, therefore, a purely contractual relation:
treated in the same way as chattels, hence the e\
of course, a lease is a property right and is cap
in land.

Chattels Personal

This category covers all other personal property a\
choses in action and choses in possession. A chos
right (it has no physical existence) which can onl
action and not by taking physical possession o\
cheque, bond, share certificate, patent and cop\
capable of being sold, pledged and transf\
tangible right that can be enjoyed by tak\
̴ e.g. a car, book, furniture and ̇

# Table of Cases

# Introductory Topics

## INTRODUCTION

English law makes a primary distinction between real and personal property (realty and personalty). Although the peculiar English history of leases provides an exception, this distinction corresponds in the main to the distinction drawn in civil law systems between immovable and movable property. A modern day significance of this distinction is that real property (or proprietary) rights have the ability to bind future purchasers of the land whereas personal rights (such as a licence) do not. The language employed, however, is difficult, technical and, at first, apt to confuse.

**Figure 1**

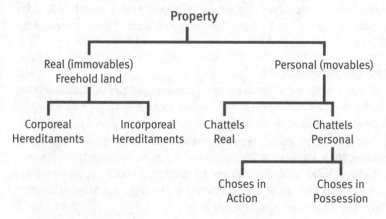

## CATEGORIES OF PROPERTY

### Real Property (Realty)

Originally, real property was the term applied to any property that was the subject matter of a real action in the common law courts. This was a right against the property (an action in rem) and was designed to ensure the return of land to a dispossessed owner. This applied only to freehold interests in land and was not available to actions relating to leaseholds.

## Corporeal and Incorporeal Hereditaments

Corporeal hereditaments are tangible, inheritable things capable of being physically possessed (i.e. the land and physical things attached to it, including any buildings thereon) and incorporeal hereditaments are inheritable rights in land which cannot be physically possessed (e.g. easements, profits and restrictive covenants).

## Personal Property (Personalty)

This relates to any property that could be made the subject of a personal action, i.e. an action against the individual rather than the property. The consequence of a personal action (for dispossession, say, of a horse) was that the wrongful dispossessor could either hand back the personal property or pay damages. With a real action, if a freeholder had been wrongly dispossessed of land then possession of the land had to be handed back.

## Leases (Chattels Real)

Historically, leases were treated as personal property simply because only a personal action could be taken for dispossession in the courts. A lease was, therefore, a purely contractual relationship. Accordingly, leases were treated in the same way as chattels, hence the expression chattels real. Today, of course, a lease is a property right and is capable of being a legal estate in land.

## Chattels Personal

This category covers all other personal property and can be subdivided into choses in action and choses in possession. A chose in action is an intangible right (it has no physical existence) which can only be claimed or enforced by action and not by taking physical possession of the thing itself, e.g. a debt, cheque, bond, share certificate, patent and copyright. Such assets are, however, capable of being sold, pledged and transferred. A chose in possession is a tangible right that can be enjoyed by taking physical possession of the thing itself, e.g. a car, book, furniture and jewellery.

### Differences and Distinctions

The classification of property as real or personal may assume significance in a number of situations. For example:

- on a testamentary disposition, e.g. when X by will leaves his realty to Y and his personalty to Z;
- a contract to dispose of personalty does not need to adhere to any prescribed form, but as regards land contracts the formalities of

s.2 of the Law of Property (Miscellaneous Provisions) Act 1989 apply and the contract must be in writing, contain all express terms and be signed by both parties;

- the purchase price paid for land will include fixtures, but does not include personal property.

## OWNERSHIP AND LAND

### Background

Since the Norman Conquest (1066) and the introduction of feudalism, the Crown technically owns all land in England. Albeit convenient, it is not, therefore, strictly correct to speak of an individual "owning" land. Instead, an individual can own only an estate in land. As will become clear in Ch.2, the quality of that ownership will vary, of course, according to the type of estate which is owned. Ownership rights, moreover, need not be vested in the same person, e.g. where a trust exists or where there are a number of different estates in the same piece of land. Consequently, it is more appropriate to deal with a person's right to possession (seisin) in determining title to land.

### DEFINITION CHECKPOINT

In the physical sense, land includes not only the ground, soil and earth, but also all buildings on the land, any fixtures attached thereto, mines and minerals and any incorporeal rights such as easements: s.205(1)(ix) of the Law of Property Act 1925. At common law the extent of ownership is said to extend up to the sky and down to the centre of the earth (*cuius est solum, eius est usque ad coelum et ad inferos*).

### *Airspace*

The airspace up to a reasonable height (as a rule of thumb between 150–200 metres above roof level) belongs to the owner: *Bernstein v Skyviews & General Ltd* (1978) and, if interfered with, may give rise to an action in trespass or nuisance: *Kelsen v Imperial Tobacco Co* (1957). Under the **Civil Aviation Act 1982**, no action can be taken in respect of aircraft that pass over property at a reasonable height. In *Anchor Brewhouse Developments Ltd v Berkley House (Docklands Developments) Ltd* (1987), an injunction was granted to prevent the jib of a crane swinging over adjoining property as this amounted to a trespass.

## Underground

Minerals and other substances in the land (such as stone, sand and gravel) at common law belong to the land owner. The depth to which ownership may sink is, however, unclear. Nevertheless, it is not as curtailed as is the case with airspace. In *Bocardo SA v Star Energy UK* (2009), a trespass occurred by the laying of pipelines over 2,000 feet below the claimant's land.

### Statutory exceptions

- water rights are governed by the **Water Resources Act 1991**. The basic rule is that a licence from the National Rivers Authority must be obtained for any extraction of water from any source, i.e. percolating or from a defined channel. No licence is required in the case of abstractions of small quantities of water for certain limited authorised purposes, e.g. domestic purposes of the occupiers household or agricultural purposes other than spray irrigation;
- rights to unworked coal vest in the Coal Authority by virtue of the **Coal Industry Act 1994**;
- rights to petroleum, mineral oil and natural gas existing in their natural state lie in the Crown under the **Petroleum Act 1998**.

### Finding property

The concept of land entails that any objects embedded in land are presumed, in the absence of the true owner, to be within the ownership of the landowner and not the finder. In *Waverley BC v Fletcher* (1995), a brooch was found below the surface of a public park with the aid of a metal detector. The Council had a better title to the brooch than did the finder whose actions amounted to a trespass. The same approach does not apply to items found lying on the surface of the land. In *Parker v British Airways Board* (1982), a bracelet was found by a passenger in an airport terminal. The passenger was able to assert a better claim than the landowner because the latter had not exerted sufficient control over the building and the things that were at any given time within it. The outcome would be different if the property was a private house as the necessary control would easily be discerned.

## Buildings

At common law "land" includes buildings as they become part of the land. As shown above, this now has statutory recognition in s.205(1)(ix) of the **Law of Property Act 1925**. In *Elitestone Ltd v Morris* (1997), the House of Lords was invited to determine whether a free-standing wooden chalet built by the tenant's predecessor in title, which rested on concrete pillars situated on the landlord's land, could be removed by the tenant to another location. The House held that it could be used only in situ and was therefore a building that formed part of the land. By way of contrast, in *Chelsea Yacht and Boat Co Ltd v Pope* (2000), a houseboat which was only slightly and temporarily attached to its mooring did not form part of the land to which it was moored. Similarly, in *Wessex Reserve Forces v White* (2006), a portable shed was not part of the land.

## Fixtures

A further rule of law is that any object that is attached to the land or a building may be categorized a fixture so as to form part of the land. Consequently when a chattel (e.g. a door or radiator) is affixed to land or to a building, it may become a fixture and thus become part of the land itself. This is of importance in deciding whether a landowner, on selling or leasing property, can remove objects from the land. The problem may also arise in connection with what property is the subject of a mortgage, devise by will or strict settlement. Although there is no decisive formula that can be applied by the courts, there are two general rules which help to distinguish a fixture from a chattel and these are the degree of annexation and purpose of annexation tests: *Holland v Hodgson* (1872).

### *Degree of annexation*

Originally, physical attachment to the land was the crucial issue. If it was attached, it was a fixture and part of the land. In modern times, the emphasis has moved away from such a rigid rule and rests now upon why the item was introduced on to the land (i.e. the purpose test). It follows, therefore, that an item can become part of the land without any attachment to the land and can remain a chattel despite secure attachment (e.g. a greenhouse: *Dean v Andrews* (1985)). The degree test is not, however, redundant. First, an absence of any physical attachment will (unless an item is so heavy that it does not require any attachment) usually entail that the item is a chattel. Secondly, the degree test may become significant where the purpose of annexation is unclear. In such cases, the extent and method of physical attachment can then give rise to a series of (sometimes even conflicting) evidential presumptions. For example, if the attachment is only slight the item is presumed not to be part of the land (say, a free standing cooker); if removal of the item will cause damage to the fabric of the building it is presumed to be a fixture (say, kitchen units); and if attachment is the only way in which the item can be enjoyed it is presumed to be a chattel (say, a heavy ornamental mirror). When the purpose test (below) is inconclusive, whichever presumption is chosen is likely to be decisive of whether an item is a fixture or not: *Hamp v Bygrave* (1983).

### Purpose of annexation

The purpose test addresses the issue of why the item was introduced on to the land. The basic question is whether the item is there in order to be a permanent improvement or is intended instead to be a temporary installation. The court here is primarily concerned with objective intentions and not the subjective intentions of the person who brought the item on to the land. The court will consider the nature of the item and the nature of its attachment to the land. Hence, some items are clearly going to be fixtures (e.g. bathroom fittings, kitchen units, doors and wall tiles) whereas others are clearly going to be chattels (e.g. lampshades, washing machines, gas fires and curtains). Fitted carpets, however, have caused some difficulties. The courts have been undecided as to whether they are to effect a permanent improvement (see *Young v Dalgety Plc* (1987) or are attached to the building merely so that they can be used (see *Botham v TSB Bank Plc* (1997). As mentioned, when the purpose is unclear, the court will resort to the degree of annexation test and the associated presumptions. Objects which form part of the architectural design of a house or grounds will be regarded as permanent fixtures whether or not they are attached. In *Re Whaley* (1908) an Elizabethan tapestry in an Elizabethan house was held to be a fixture. Similarly, in *D'Eyncourt v Gregory* (1866) freestanding ornaments were regarded as fixtures because they formed an integral part of the landscaped garden.

### Removal

In the absence of contrary agreement, the general rule is that if an item constitutes a fixture it cannot be removed from the land. Accordingly, a vendor must leave fixtures for a purchaser. In relation to landlord and tenant (similar rules apply also as between tenant for life and remainderman) there are limited exceptions. A tenant may remove certain "tenants fixtures" either during the lease or within a reasonable time thereafter. These include:

- trade fixtures (i.e. items attached by the tenant for the purpose of a trade or business);
- ornamental and domestic fixtures (e.g. blinds, stoves and grates); and
- agricultural fixtures provided that an opportunity to purchase them is first given to the landlord.

## LAND USE AND THE EUROPEAN CONVENTION ON HUMAN RIGHTS

### Background

The Human Rights Act 1998 incorporates the European Convention into English law. The latter identifies a series of fundamental rights and freedoms which are central to the proper treatment of the individual within society. Since the 1998 Act, domestic legislation must be interpreted in a fashion that is compatible with the Convention rights. The Convention rights bind the state, local authorities, courts and tribunals. The rights are not, however, absolute and may be overridden if their disregard is warranted by domestic law and is in the wider public interest. There must be an objective and reasonable justification for a departure. A principle of proportionality operates here which means that there must be a balance between the interference and the furtherance of a social interest.

### What Human Rights?
*Article 1*

This contains a guarantee of property rights (i.e. substantive rights) by offering:

- freedom from arbitrary deprivation of possessions (which can include tenancy rights, for example);
- freedom from unjustified controls on the use of property; and
- peaceful enjoyment of possessions.

*Article 6*

This offers a right to a fair trial of, say, property disputes. This concerns only procedure and not the substantive law as applied by the courts.

*Article 8*

This gives a right to respect for a person's home and family life. Article 8 does not require the state to offer security of tenure to a surviving relative of a tenant nor does it offer a right to be provided with a home: *Chapman v United Kingdom* (2001). It is concerned with rights to privacy and does not, for example, prevent the eviction of an individual by an owner of land (*Harrow LBC v Qazi* (2004)) or the overreaching of a beneficial interest by a mortgagee (*National Westminster Bank Plc v Malhan* (2004)). As the law currently stands, rights given under domestic law cannot be defeated by some pleading of an individual's personal plight: *Kay v Lambeth LBC* (2006).

*Article 14*

This offers freedom from discrimination in the exercise of Convention rights. Article 14 is directed at the enjoyment of other freestanding Convention rights. It does not operate independently. The discrimination must, moreover, be grounded upon a personal difference (e.g. sex, race, colour, language or personal status). In *Ghaidan v Godin-Mendoza* (2004), the discrimination alleged concerned the more favourable treatment of heterosexual couples under the Rent Act 1977 than that which was afforded to same sex couples. This statutory provision fell squarely within art. 8 and, therefore, art. 14 was engaged because of the discriminatory nature of the provision. The House of Lords could see no legitimate justification for this difference in treatment and reinterpreted the provision so as to give equal rights to all couples.

## Revision Checklist

You should now know and understand:

- **the various classifications of property;**
- **what is meant by the term "land";**
- **how to distinguish a fixture from a chattel;**
- **the possible impact of human rights law.**

## QUESTION AND ANSWER

### Question

James enters into a contract to purchase the freehold of Africa House. The building is fitted throughout with expensive carpets, luxurious wood paneling and exotic wall tapestries. The trophy room contains a rare collection of stuffed creatures, some of which are displayed in ornate wall cabinets. The grounds are styled to resemble an African village and feature free-standing traditional huts and statues of native warriors. Kirk wishes to remove the above named items.

    Advise Kirk.

### Advice and the Answer

This problem question is about the legal status of objects introduced on to land and, more particularly, the distinction between fixtures and chattels. It is to be appreciated that if the items are classified as fixtures then, unless provided otherwise in the contract, they must be left for the purchaser. Fixtures are part of the land and are paid for in the purchase price for the land. If items are classified as chattels, they do not become part of the land, are not paid for in the purchase price and can be removed by Kirk.

It is necessary to consider the two primary tests employed to identify what is and what is not a fixture, namely the degree of annexation test and the purpose of annexation test. These should be applied in turn. Accordingly, in relation to the stuffed creatures (whether attached or otherwise), common sense dictates that such artefacts cannot be said to form part of the land. Hence, these items remain chattels. As regards the other items, it is helpful to look at the physical attachment (if any) of them to the land. In the case of the carpets, paneling, tapestries and cabinets there is, seemingly, a high degree of physical attachment to the floors and walls of the building. Following *Holland v Hodgson*, therefore, it is to be presumed that these items are fixtures. The burden of proof will, therefore, shift to Kirk to show that they remain chattels. In relation to the items which are unattached, the *Holland v Hodgson* approach gives rise to the evidential presumption that the huts and statues are chattels. The burden, therefore, rests with James to prove otherwise.

Turning to the purpose of annexation test, it is to be accepted that, in modern times, this is the key yardstick to be employed. The crucial issue is why a particular item was brought on to the land. If it is to make a permanent improvement, the item will be a fixture even if there is no physical attachment whatsoever: *Dean v Andrews*. If, instead, it is designed to be a temporary improvement, or physical attachment was necessary in order for the item to be used or stabilized, then the item will be classified as a chattel: *Botham v TSB*. As to the items attached to the land (carpets, paneling, tapestries and cabinets), it would seem that the paneling will clearly be viewed as an improvement to the land and classified as a fixture. It would damage the fabric of the building to remove this paneling. The tapestries are likely to be mere wall hangings (e.g. akin to paintings, pictures and mirrors) and, despite a degree of annexation, to be viewed as chattels. As discussed below, this advice would change, however, if they form part of the grand design of Africa House: *Re Whaley*. Previous cases have demonstrated that, in relation to fitted carpets, the court has struggled to make a clear determination (see *Young v Dalgety Plc*). In one sense, it can be argued that minimum attachment is necessary so that the carpets can be safely used and that their removal will not damage the fabric of the building. These arguments point towards the carpets remaining chattels. An alternative submission could be that the carpets are intended to mark a long term improvement to the building and should, therefore, be viewed as fixtures. Much depends upon the perceptions of the court: *Hamp v Bygrave*. The cabinets will be securely attached to the walls and appear to be an integral part of the trophy room. They are likely to be regarded as fixtures. Even the free-standing huts and statues will be classified as fixtures if they form part of the architectural design of the house or garden: *D'Eyncourt v Gregory*. In view of the elaborate landscaping of Africa House, it is strongly arguable that the items were brought on to the land to effect a permanent improvement and are, therefore, fixtures.

# Tenures and Estates

......................................................................................................................

## 2

## THE DOCTRINE OF TENURES

### Introduction

From the time of the Norman Conquest (1066), English land law adopted the continental system of feudalism which embodied a hierarchy dominated by a paramount lord, the King, and based on mutual promises between lords and their subordinates (vassals) of protection and military service. William the Conqueror (1066–87) regarded the whole of England as his by conquest and granted land, not by out and out transfer, but to be held of him as overlord. This is known as allodial or prerogative ownership. Persons holding land of the Crown might then grant land to another (subinfeudation) to hold of him in return for services. The feudal pyramid that was constructed was based upon a system of land tenure. The person in possession at the bottom of the feudal pyramid was called the tenant in demesne and those between him and the King were termed mesne lords. The tenure of the land identified the conditions on which land was held. These varied in terms of nature and status. Tenure was the main bond holding society together, the lord protecting those who held land of him. It is now, however, largely of historical interest.

### Forms of Tenure
#### *Free tenures*

These were when the nature of the duties was fixed, and the services were rendered freely. The most common types of free tenure were:

- chivalry such as knight's service (military service in return for land) and sergeantry (personal services for the lord);
- socage, which primarily involved the provision of agricultural services of a fixed nature; and
- spiritual tenure such as frankalmoin and divine service, which involved grants to ecclesiastical bodies in return for the saying of prayers or masses for the repose of the soul and/or spiritual well-being of the feudal lord.

*Unfree tenures*

Unfree tenures included villeinage and copyhold which were labour intensive services, often agricultural, but were not fixed in nature and amount. By the 14th century, these were commuted to payment of rent, enabling the lord to hire labour independently.

### Incidents of Tenure

As part of the tenure system the lord was entitled to certain incidents which were often of great value to him. These varied with the different types of tenure held. The most common incidents were:

- homage, fealty and suit of court which involved the tenant swearing to be the lord's man and to perform the feudal obligations as well as agreeing to attend the lord's court;
- relief which amounted to the payment of money to the lord when the tenant died;
- aids, which were special payments required when the lord needed ransom or the eldest son was knighted or his daughter needed dowry;
- escheat and forfeiture, which occurred where the land passed to the lord because of failure of heirs or where the tenant committed a serious crime (felony);
- wardship, which gave to the lord the right to retain profits from the land where an infant succeeded to the tenancy (under the age of 21 for a male and 14 years for a female); and
- marriage, which gave the lord the right to select the spouse of a tenant.

### Remnants of Tenure

In general, the doctrine of tenures has no practical effect today. The **Tenures Abolition Act 1660** effectively destroyed all lay tenures except for socage (freehold tenure as it is usually termed) and copyhold (originally an unfree tenure acquired by serfs in return for their labour). The **Law of Property Act 1922** abolished copyhold and, except socage, all other incidents of tenure. Consequently, there remains only one form of tenure, i.e. socage. It is now assumed that a landowner holds land as tenant in chief directly from the Crown, but without the provision of services. On sale, the purchaser replaces the vendor as tenant in chief.

## THE DOCTRINE OF ESTATES

### Introduction

Whereas the doctrine of tenures dealt with the conditions on which land was held, the doctrine of estates is concerned with the length of time for which land is held. As all land in England is held of the Crown, English law has developed the concept of the estate which has its emphasis on the right to possession (seisin) and not ownership. Estates represent a stake or slice of time in land and, as such, are an abstract entitlement which represents the extent of a person's rights to possession. Reduced to its basics, an estate represents the temporal quality of ownership in land, i.e. the estate reflects the extent of the right of seisin. A person may be entitled to seisin in perpetuity or for a limited period of time. As explained in Walsingham's case (1573), "an estate in the land is a time in the land, or land for a time, and there are diversities of estates, which are no more than diversities of time".

## Classification of Estates

As indicated, estates vary in size according to their potential duration. The general nature of these estates is considered below and they are also considered further at appropriate places in the text. There are two principal categories of estate: freehold and less than freehold (which now means leasehold). A freehold estate (originally derived from the law of tenures) is one whose duration is uncertain, whereas an estate less than freehold is one for a period whose duration is fixed or capable of being fixed (e.g. a lease for 10 years).

Figure 2

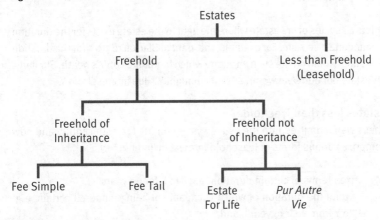

## Freehold Estates
### *Fee simple*

This is the largest estate in terms of duration (it is potentially infinite in duration) and is as near to "absolute ownership" as it is possible to achieve under English land law. The word *fee* connotes inheritability and *simple* indicates that right to inherit is unrestricted (i.e. it is inheritable by general heirs whether ascendants or descendants). The fee simple is virtually everlasting in that it continues as long as the person entitled for the time being has "heirs" left to inherit. The classic words of limitation used to create such an estate are "to (X) and his heirs".

### Fee tail

This is an inheritable estate (lesser in quantum than the fee simple) which lasts for as long as the original grantee or any of his lineal descendants live. The terms fee tail, estate tail, entail or entailed interest are often used to describe the same style of estate. A classic method of creation was to use the words "to (X) and the heirs of his body". A restriction of the line of descendants to the male or female species only could be created by a fee tail male or a fee tail female. Following the Trusts of Land and Appointment of Trustees Act 1996, it is no longer possible to create an entailed interest. Any attempt to do so will produce a trust for the grantee absolutely.

### Life estate

This arises where there is a grant of an estate to the grantee for his life. The estate is not inheritable and, since the **Law of Property Act 1925**, can only exist as an equitable estate behind a trust of land.

### Estate pur autre vie

This is a species of life estate where the right to the estate exists for the duration of someone else's life. For example, the grant of Blackacre "to X for the duration of Y's life" would create such an estate which terminates on Y's death. Similarly, an estate pur autre vie would arise if X bought Y's life interest from Y.

## Estates less than Freehold

These were admitted into the estate system during the 16th century and now comprise various forms of leasehold interest including:

- fixed terms of certain duration, e.g. "to X for 99 years";
- a term the duration of which is capable of being rendered certain, e.g. "to Y from year to year"; and
- a tenancy at will which has been described as the lowest estate known to the law.

## Estates in Possession, Remainder and Reversion

A further consequence of the concept of the "estate" is that the law allows various smaller and simultaneous estates to be carved out of the fee simple estate: e.g. "to A for life then to B in fee simple". The following observations need to be made:

- in the grant "to A for life then to B in fee simple", the estate of B is an estate in remainder, i.e. B does not have a present right to actual enjoyment and B's right to possession is postponed to the future;
- an estate vests both in interest and in possession where a present right to immediate enjoyment is given, e.g. there is no preceding estate to postpone enjoyment. In the preceding example, A's prior life interest has vested on both levels (i.e. A has the right to the present enjoyment and use of the property);
- while A remains alive, B's estate is one vested in interest only. The interest is not vested in possession because B does not have a present right to use and enjoyment of the property; and where land will revert back to the original grantor, then the grantor has an estate in reversion so that if Blackacre is simply conveyed by X "to A for life", then the estate of X is a reversion.

## RIGHTS OF A FEE SIMPLE OWNER

The fee simple being the largest estate that can exist in land carries with it many of the rights which would be associated with absolute ownership of property. These include:

### Natural Rights
There is a natural right of support for land (although not for buildings where such rights must be acquired by easement or covenant) and a natural right to an unpolluted free flow of air across property. These rights exist automatically and do not require any form of grant.

### Right of Alienation
A fee simple owner may dispose of his land in any way he chooses, either by deed or by will.

### Right of Enjoyment
The rights of enjoyment possessed by a fee simple owner are extensive. In physical terms he may enjoy everything on, beneath and above the land but, as shown in Ch.1, there are practical restrictions to this rule. In addition to what was considered in the preceding chapter, the right of enjoyment may be compromised by the property rights of others. For example, a third party might have an easement to cross the land, a restrictive covenant to prevent building on the land or the right to occupy the land by virtue of a lease. In exercising rights

over land, moreover, the fee simple owner must not interfere with the legal rights of other landowners.

## Fishing Rights

In non-tidal waters the owner has the exclusive right to fish and this right may be granted to others, e.g. fishing clubs. In tidal water, the public has a right to fish up to the point of ebb and flow of the tide.

## Wild Animals

Wild animals cannot, while living, form the subject matter of ownership, but a fee simple owner has a qualified right to catch, kill and appropriate. Certain species of animals and birds are, however, protected by statute, e.g. the **Wildlife and Countryside Act 1981**.

## Statutory restrictions

Statutory restrictions have eroded away certain rights of an owner. Many of these statutes are based on public interest and illustrate public authority interference, e.g. the **Town and Country Planning Acts**; the **Rent Acts**; and a variety of **Housing and Public Health Acts**.

## Items Found on the Land

As shown in Ch. 1, a distinction is here to be drawn between lost items found on the surface of the land and items which are found under, attached to or embedded in the land. As regards surface objects, the finder has a better claim to the item unless the landowner has exerted sufficient control over the land and things which might be found on it. The finder will otherwise have a good title which can be defeated only by the true owner of the item. If the item is found either under, in or attached to the land, the landowner has a better claim than the finder does: *Waverley BC v Fletcher* (1995).

## Treasure Trove

Treasure trove is subject to the **Treasure Act 1996**. When treasure is found it will usually vest in the Crown. Coroners may hold inquests to determine whether items found constitute treasure, but in most cases without a jury. The Secretary of State has produced a code of practice for dealing with rewards to finders of treasure. The definition of treasure includes:

- objects (other than single coins) at least 300 years old which comprise of at least 10 per cent precious metal;
- finds of 10 or more coins of any metal which are at least 300 years old; and

- other items that are at least 200 years old and which are designated by the Secretary of State as being of outstanding historical, archaeological or cultural importance.

Revision Checklist

You should now know and understand:

- the major types of tenure and their limited modern day significance;

- the concept of an estate;

- the different types of estate;

- the rights and entitlements of a fee simple owner.

# QUESTION AND ANSWER

## Question

What is tenure, does it enjoy any modern day value and how does it differ from an estate in land?

## Advice and the Answer

This is a straightforward essay style question and it requires an equally straightforward answer. In the medieval period, tenures and estates were two key mechanisms by which land was held. A person would hold land on tenure for the duration of his estate. It is, therefore, necessary to consider the meaning of both concepts through the eyes of history.

The basic principle of feudal landholding was that land was allocated in return for services (e.g. of an agricultural or military nature). The type of service which was provided in return for land was called "tenure". Accordingly, "tenure" represented the conditions under which land was held. All land was held directly from the King and a tiered network was built up by those under the king creating lesser interests to persons of lower rank. The end of tenure was signaled by the **Tenures Abolition Act 1660** and the process was completed by the **Law of Property Act 1922**. Indeed, the only relic of tenure remaining today is "socage" which reflects

TENURES AND ESTATES

17

the fact that all land is deemed to held from the Crown, but no services are nowadays provided.

Whereas tenure is to do with conditions attached to land holding, the concept of the "estate" is to do with duration. As the Crown is the institutional "owner" of land, individuals can only own an estate in land. There are two types of estate that can exist at law: the freehold (the "fee simple") and the leasehold. The former is in perpetuity whereas the latter is of a limited lifespan (e.g. 99 years). The freehold estate is, therefore, better than its leasehold counterpart. These estates are of key contemporary importance and it is to be noted that there can be different estates in land existing at the same time. For example, a freeholder of a house may grant a five year lease to a tenant. Each will have their respective rights in relation to the land.

# Law and Equity

## 3

## INTRODUCTION

The term equity is, in a general sense, associated with notions of fairness, morality and justice. It is an ethical jurisdiction. On a more practical level, however, equity is the branch of law that was administered in the Court of Chancery prior to the Judicature Acts 1873 and 1875. This was a jurisdiction evolved to achieve justice and to overcome the rigours and deficiencies of the common law, i.e. delay, complicated procedures of the writ system and inadequate remedies. It is in the realms of property law that equity has arguably made its greatest contribution.

## DEVELOPMENTS OF EQUITY

The Trust

### DEFINITION CHECKPOINT

At common law, it was not possible to have an enforceable arrangement under which one person would hold the legal title of property for the benefit of another. The common law was preoccupied with legal title only. Equity intervened to allow such an arrangement in the form of the trust (originally called a use). The common denominator of all trusts is that legal title (i.e. nominal, paper title) to the property is held by trustees whereas equitable or beneficial (substantive) ownership is vested in the beneficiary.

#### Characteristics

The existence of a trust is dependent upon identifiable property (whether tangible or intangible) being transferred from its legal owner to one or more trustees to hold and manage property for the benefit of ascertainable beneficiaries. The trust may be created inter vivos (i.e. during the lifetime of the settlor) or may be post-mortem (i.e on the death of the settlor). The trustee labours under the duty to protect the trust assets and to distribute trust income and capital in accordance with the terms of the trust. The trustee, therefore, owes an equitable, fiduciary obligation of good faith and loyalty and must always act to the benefit of the beneficiaries. If the trustee fails to do so, he will be personally liable for his breach of trust. In general terms, therefore, a trust is either a self-imposed obligation, or an obligation imposed on a third party (in whom legal title to the property becomes vested), to act for the benefit of another which is enforceable in equity. The equitable interest in property thereby becomes different and distinct form the nominal legal ownership vested in the trustee.

**Figure 3: The Trust Relationship**

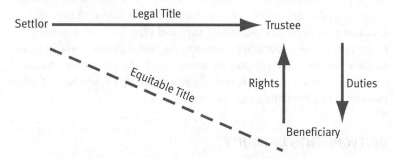

### Equitable Right to Redeem
This is the right of a mortgagor (borrower) to redeem the mortgage loan (by payment of capital, interest and costs) even after the legal (i.e. contractual) date for redemption has passed (see Ch.12). Equity is vigilant to ensure that the right to redeem is not subject to clogs and fetters or rendered illusory by contractual provisions imposed on the borrower.

### Burden of Restrictive Covenants
A covenant is a contractual agreement and, as with all contracts, the benefit of the contract may be assigned to a third party. At common law, however, only a party to the contract/covenant could be held liable. This shortcoming in the law of covenants was, in part, mitigated by equity in allowing the burden of a restrictive freehold covenant (i.e. a negative covenant) to run with the land in equity and, thereby, bind future purchasers of the burdened land. This development is usually traced back to the decision in *Tulk v Moxhay* (1848). It still remains the case that the burden of a positive covenant cannot run with the land.

### Equitable Remedies
Equity developed a series of discretionary remedies (i.e. remedies which cannot be claimed as of right) in order to overcome the inadequacy of the common law damages. These include:

## Injunctions

An injunction is an order of the court which requires a person either to do something (i.e. a positive or mandatory injunction) or, more commonly, to refrain from doing something (i.e. a negative or prohibitory injunction). Damages may be awarded in lieu of, or in addition to, an injunction. There are various types of injunction, each of which has been designed to achieve a different function.

### *Specific performance*

Specific performance is an order of the court which directs the defendant to perform his side of a contract. Specific performance operates in relation to the entire contract and not merely a part of the agreement. The remedy will not be granted if damages would adequately compensate the claimant. An example of where specific performance will readily be granted concerns contracts for the sale of land. This is because each piece of land is considered to be unique and damages will not normally be sufficient to compensate a potential purchaser. Although damages may be suitable for the vendor, a need for mutuality also allows the vendor to claim specific performance of a land contract. Specific performance is not, however, available for all types of contract. As regards contracts for the sale of goods, such as a car or a television, specific performance will not usually be an appropriate remedy.

### *Rescission*

Rescission is a remedy employed to set aside a contract and to restore the parties to their pre-contractual positions. The contract is, therefore, voidable and, until rescinded, remains perfectly valid. Accordingly, rescission reflects the desire of one party no longer to be bound by the contract. Equity claims the ability to set aside a contract where the transaction is tainted by what is known as a vitiating factor. The grounds for rescission include for example, misrepresentation, undue influence and breach of fiduciary duty.

### *Rectification*

The remedy of rectification concerns the rewriting of documents to accord with what the parties agreed in bilateral transactions (such as contracts) or, in the case of a voluntary deed (such as a trust), with what the settlor truly intended. The remedy is, therefore, designed to rectify mistakes made. Although it is a discretionary remedy, rectification will usually be awarded unless damages offer a suitable alternative. Rectification most commonly occurs when a term is omitted from a written contract due to a mutual mistake of the parties. Rectification for a unilateral mistake can, however, occur, but only when there has been fraud, unconscionable behaviour or some other sharp practice by the other party: *Thomas Bates & Son Ltd v Wyndham's (Lingerie) Ltd* (1981).

## LEGAL AND EQUITABLE RIGHTS

### DEFINITION CHECKPOINT

A legal right is a right in rem (in the thing itself) which is automatically binding upon the entire world. An equitable right, however, is a right in personam. Hence, it has a more limited capacity to bind third parties. Absent any registration requirements, it will not bind a bona fide purchaser for value of a legal estate without notice of the equitable interest (equity's darling). Although both are property rights, an equitable right is, traditionally, inferior to its legal counterpart.

### Is it legal?

In order for a right to be legal it must:

* be listed in s.1(2) of the **Law of Property Act 1925** as having the potential to be legal. This list includes charges by way of legal mortgage, easements, rent charges and rights of entry. Any other right must necessarily be equitable: s.1(3). This means that restrictive covenants, estoppel rights and interests under a trust of land must always be equitable interests;
* the right must also equate with a freehold or leasehold estate (and not, say, with a life interest); and
* the right must, as a general rule, be granted by a formal document known as a deed: s.52(1) of the **Law of Property Act 1925**. Equitable interests expressly created need only be created in writing: s.53(1)(a).

### Example

A and B are adjoining landowners. B grants to A the permanent right to cross his land in order to reach a main road. A has an easement over B's land. As an easement is a right listed in s.1(2), if it is created by deed it will be a legal easement. If it is created merely in writing, then it must be an equitable easement. If B sells his land to C, the purchaser will, at common law, automatically be bound by a legal easement because it is a right enforceable against all persons. If the easement is equitable, the doctrine of notice is the traditional mechanism used to determine whether the right binds C.

## The Doctrine of Notice
### *Meaning*

The basic doctrine of notice provides that an equitable interest will bind all persons other than equity's darling, i.e. the bona fide purchaser for value of the legal estate with no notice of the equitable interest, or anyone who claims through him: *Pilcher v Rawlins* (1872). The impact and effect of the doctrine of notice has, however, been considerably reduced by legislation. As regards unregistered land, it has been substantially replaced by a system of land charges registration. The doctrine of notice does, however, retain a limited, residual role (see Ch.6). As regards registered land (see Ch.7), however, the traditional view is that the doctrine of notice has no relevance whatsoever (*Midland Bank v Green* (1980)).

**Figure 4**

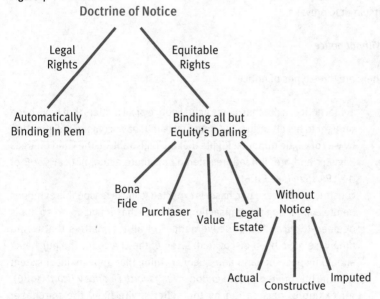

Doctrine of Notice

### *Bona fide*

The purchaser must act in good faith, i.e. there must be no fraud or sharp practice: *Midland Bank v Green* (1980). Usually, however, this condition merely emphasises that the purchaser must be innocent as to notice.

### *Purchaser*

This includes any person who takes the property by sale, mortgage, will, lease or otherwise, but excludes any acquisition by operation of law (e.g. under the intestacy rules).

*Value*

This includes any consideration for money or money's worth or marriage (i.e. an ante-nuptial settlement of property). The consideration need not be adequate and can even be at an under value. Natural love and affection will not suffice. Inheriting under a will does not amount to value.

*Legal estate*

The estate purchased must be a legal estate which includes freehold, leasehold and, by virtue of statute, a mortgage. If the purchaser only acquires an equitable estate he will not, therefore, take free of prior equitable interests. In that situation, equity operates on the principle that where the equities are equal the first in time prevails.

*Without notice*

There are three types of notice:

- actual notice: a purchaser has actual notice of all matters that have been brought to his attention, but not of facts that have come to his attention by way of vague rumours. Rights that are registrable in the Land Charges Register and are, indeed, registered constitute actual notice: s.198 of the LPA 1925 (see Ch.6);
- constructive notice: a purchaser is expected to make reasonable enquiries before completing the transaction. If the purchaser fails to do so, he is deemed to have "constructive notice" of all the matters that would otherwise have been discovered: s.199 of the LPA 1925. The purchaser should inspect the land and query anything that appears inconsistent with the title offered by the vendor. In *Kingsnorth Finance v Tizard* (1986), for example, occupation by the seller's wife fixed the purchaser with constructive notice of her equitable rights in the property. This was so even though the husband lied and tried to hide traces of her occupation; and
- imputed notice: where a purchaser employs an agent, such as a solicitor or surveyor, any notice (whether actual or constructive) attributed to the agent is imputed to the purchaser. In the *Kingsnorth Finance* case, the constructive notice of an agent surveyor was imputed to the purchaser (the mortgagee). The agent must, however, be employed by the purchaser at the time when the actual or constructive notice is acquired: *Halifax Building Society v Stepsky* (1997).

Once an equitable right is defeated by a bona fide purchaser for value of a legal estate without notice of the equitable interest, it entirely loses the ability to bind third parties. It cannot be resurrected and cannot, therefore, bind a future purchaser even if that purchaser knows of the existence of the right: *Wilkes v Spooner* (1911).

## Revision Checklist

You should now know and understand:

- the impact of equity and, in particular, the nature of a trust and types of equitable remedies;

- the difference between legal and equitable rights;

- the types of legal right and how they are created;

- the scope and operation of the doctrine of notice.

# QUESTION AND ANSWER

## Question

Chris is intending to purchase the unregistered freehold of "the Lodge" for £200,000 from Terry. Although Terry is the sole legal owner, he lives in "the Lodge" with his wife, Margaret. She has a beneficial interest in the property. Unfortunately, Margaret recently had a car accident and has been in hospital for the last 12 weeks. She does not know that Terry is intending to sell "the Lodge" and to move (with the proceeds of sale) to Spain. Chris visited the premises last month and was assured by Terry that he was the sole owner and occupier of "the Lodge". Chris' solicitor, Emma, is Margaret's sister.

Terry's neighbour, Jim, has the benefit of a legal easement over "the Lodge" which allows him to cross the land as a short cut to the local village. This right was granted by a previous owner of "the Lodge".

On the assumption that the rights of the parties are governed solely by the doctrine of notice, advise Chris whether on completion of the transaction he will be bound by the interests of Margaret and Jim.

## Advice and the Answer

The assumption required at the end of the question entails that you are not to discuss land charges and land registration. Albeit somewhat artificial, this is purely a question concerning the doctrine of notice as a mechanism for resolving property disputes.

The starting point is to make the fundamental distinction between legal interests and equitable interests. Legal interests are those rights listed in s.1(2) of the **Law of Property Act 1925** and which, as a general rule, are created by deed (s.52). An easement is within the s.1(2) list and the right of way in favour of Jim is (you are told) a legal right. Jim's land, therefore, has the benefit a legal easement over "the Lodge". A beneficial interest under a trust of land is not, however, listed in s.1(2) and, therefore, can exist only as an equitable interest in land (s.1(3)). Accordingly, Margaret's interest is merely equitable.

As regards the doctrine of notice, there are two key propositions. First, legal interests bind the world automatically (i.e. they bind in rem). Hence, Chris will be bound by Jim's legal easement if the purchase goes ahead. As regards equitable rights, the rule is that they will bind everyone with the exception of "equity's darling" (i.e. the bona fide purchaser of the legal estate for value without notice). Hence, Margaret's beneficial interest will only bind Chris if he does not fall within this descriptive label. Looking at the transaction, Chris is a prospective "purchaser" for value (£200,000) of the freehold "legal estate". There is no suggestion that he is anything other than a bona fide purchaser and no evidence of any bad faith or sharp practice. The main issue concerns whether Chris had notice of Margaret's property interest. It does not appear that he had actual notice (i.e. he did not subjectively know of her beneficial interest). Nevertheless, he is likely to have both constructive and imputed notice of her rights. Constructive notice covers that which Chris should objectively know (i.e. what a purchaser making reasonable enquiries would have discovered). Admittedly, he visited the premises and saw no evidence of Margaret's occupation. Nevertheless, following *Kingsnorth Finance v Tizard* this will not offer Chris protection. The law expects Chris to go further and, for example, to search the electoral roll or to ask neighbours. As Chris did not take these precautionary steps, he will take subject to Margaret's beneficial interest. The fact that Margaret is in hospital serves to explain why she was not at "the Lodge" when Chris visited the property. Her hospitalisation does not affect the binding nature of her trust interest nor does it impact upon the notion of constructive notice.

The final aspect here concerns the role of Emma. She is, it will be recalled, both Chris' solicitor and Margaret's sister. In her latter capacity, she is likely to know that Margaret lives in "the Lodge" and that Margaret may well have an interest in the property. If so, this will constitute actual notice which may be imputed to her client, Chris. It is knowledge which she has while acting as solicitor for Chris and, accordingly, may be transferred to her client.

In conclusion, Chris will be bound by Jim's legal easement and also, due to constructive notice and (possibly) imputed notice, will purchase the legal estate subject to Margaret's trust interest.

# Estates and Interests

## 4

## INTRODUCTION

In 1925, there was a systematic overhaul of property law. A raft of legislation was passed in that year which included the **Law of Property Act**; the **Settled Land Act**; the **Trustee Act**; the **Administration of Estates Act**; the **Land Charges Act** (now 1972); and the **Land Registration Act** (now 2002). The legislation achieved the following general effects:

- it limited the effects of the tenure system and reduced the number of tenures to a common form, i.e. socage (see Ch. 2);
- it reduced the number of legal estates in land to two and the number of legal interests to five;
- it extended the system of registration of charges and registration of title;
- it abandoned many outmoded rules and modernised what had become an antiquated system; and
- it facilitated the cheaper conveyancing of land.

## REDUCTION OF LEGAL ESTATES AND INTERESTS

### Two Legal Estates
In an attempt to simplify conveyancing and to assist a purchaser of land, one of the principal innovations of the **Law of Property Act 1925** was to reduce the number of legal estates that may exist in land. Section 1(1) provides that the only estates in land which can now be legal are the fee simple absolute in possession and the term of years absolute.

### Four Legal Interests
Section 1(2) further provides that there are now five legal interests in or over land:

- an easement, right or privilege in or over land equivalent to an estate in fee simple absolute in possession or a term of years absolute;

- a rentcharge in possession issued out of or charged on land being either perpetual or for a term of years absolute;
- a charge expressed to be by way of legal mortgage;
- a statutory charge; and
- rights of entry exercisable over or in respect of a legal term of years absolute, or annexed, for any purpose, to a legal rentcharge.

## Listed or not?

It follows that, if an estate or interest is not within these listed categories, it must necessarily be equitable: s.1(3) of the **LPA 1925**. For example, a life estate is an equitable estate. Restrictive covenants and trust interests are equitable interests. If within the statutory lists, the estate or interest merely has the potential to be legal. As to whether it is legal or not, it is necessary to consider how the estate or interest was created. This is because the general rule is that, for a legal estate or legal interest to exist, it must be created formally by deed: s.52(1) of the **LPA**. For example, an easement granted merely in writing can only be equitable. An exception to the rule, however, lies with leases not exceeding three years which can be legal even if granted in writing or, indeed, orally: s.54(2).

> The difference between an "estate" and an "interest" is that an estate represents the quality of ownership (and brings with it rights to possess and deal with the land) whereas an interest is merely a right over someone else's land (e.g. to cross the other's land or to prevent building on that land).

## FEE SIMPLE ABSOLUTE IN POSSESSION

### DEFINITION CHECKPOINT

This freehold estate has already been discussed in Ch.2 and, it will be recalled, it is an estate of inheritance that lasts as long as the "owner" has heirs. The word "absolute" is used to distinguish a fee simple that may continue forever from the concept of a modified fee.

### Modified Fees

There are three types of modified fee:

#### The determinable fee

This is a fee simple which will end automatically on the happening of a specified event. For example, "to X in fee simple until the church tower of St Paul's cathedral falls down" or "to X in fee simple until his bankruptcy". It is not certain that the event will ever occur. Not being absolute, this type of fee simple cannot be a legal estate.

### A fee simple on condition subsequent

This is a fee simple which is liable to cease if a condition is broken. If the event ever occurs the grantor has a right of re-entry, but the estate does not automatically terminate. For example, "to X in fee simple on condition that the church tower on St Paul's cathedral never falls down" or "to X in fee simple, but if he becomes bankrupt then to Y absolutely".

### A fee simple on condition precedent

This is a fee simple which will commence on a particular event, e.g. "to X and his heirs when he reaches the age of 30".

## Differences and Distinctions

The difference between a determinable fee and a fee simple on condition subsequent is not easy to identify. The major distinction lies in the words used to connect the fee simple to the contingent event:

- whenever the words set the limit for the estate first granted, it is determinable, for example, "until", "while", "during" or "as long as";
- where the words form a grant subject to the possibility of it being defeated then a fee simple on condition subsequent is created, for example, "provided that", "on condition that", "if it happens that" and "but if";
- the importance of the distinction is that, while the determinable fee can only exist in equity behind a trust (it not being "absolute" for the purposes of s.1), it is possible for a fee simple on condition subsequent to be "absolute". The **Law of Property Act 1925** states that a fee simple subject to a legal or equitable right of entry or re-entry is for statutory purposes to be treated as if it were a fee simple absolute.

## Void Conditions

If the condition attached to a determinable fee is rendered void, the whole grant fails. If, however, the estate is a conditional fee and the condition is rendered void, this creates a fee simple absolute and only the condition is invalidated. For this reason the courts are much stricter in construing conditional fees than they are in construing determinable fees based on the same type of condition.

*A condition may be void because*

- it is too vague. In *Re Jones* (1953), a condition that the donee should not have a social or other relationship with a certain named person was void for uncertainty;
- it prevents alienation. A provision which entirely prevents the sale of the land will be void: *Hood v Oglander* (1865). A partial restraint may, however, be valid: *Re Macleay* (1875);
- it purports to exclude operation of bankruptcy laws: *Re Machu* (1882);
- it is in total restraint of marriage: *Clayton v Ramsden* (1943). A partial restraint may be valid as in *Re Tepper's Will Trusts* (1986) where a reference to marrying outside "the Jewish faith" was a permissible condition; and
- it is contrary to public policy. Any provision that encourages immorality, illegality, the breakdown of marriage or the family will be inoperative.

## In Possession

The term "in possession" in s.1(1)(a) is used to distinguish present enjoyment from future enjoyment. A grant to "A for life; remainder to B in fee simple" does not give B a legal estate. Instead B's estate is equitable. Possession includes receipt of rent and profits of land, or the right to receive them: s.205(1)(xix) of the **LPA 1925**. Hence, a fee simple owner who has leased his land remains a legal estate owner despite no longer having physical possession.

## A TERM OF YEARS ABSOLUTE (THE LEASEHOLD ESTATE)

> **DEFINITION CHECKPOINT**
>
> This is the other legal estate in land recognised by the **LPA 1925**. It is a legal estate of fixed duration and includes a lease of less than a year, or for a year or years or a fraction of a year, or from year to year: s.205(1)(xxvii) of the **LPA**. It includes periodic tenancies.

## Meaning of Absolute

The term "absolute" has little significance here as s.205 of the **LPA** provides that a term of years will still be absolute even though it may be prematurely terminated, e.g. by notice to quit, landlord's re-entry or surrender by the tenant.

## Reversionary Leases

There is no requirement that the lease should be in possession; it may commence in the future (this is known as a "reversionary lease"). Nevertheless, s.149 of the **LPA** makes most reversionary leases void if they are to take effect more than 21 years from the date of the instrument of creation.

## LEGAL INTERESTS

**Figure 5**

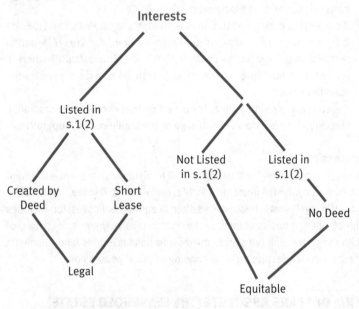

### Easements, Rights and Privileges

An easement is essentially a right to do something on another's land. The reference to rights and privileges will cover profits a prendre (e.g. a right to remove fish or crops from the land), but not a restrictive covenant.

### Rentcharges

A rentcharge is a right to a periodical sum of money (other than under a lease or mortgage) secured on land. For example, when A charges his freehold land in favour of B with the annual payment of £500, B has a rentcharge over A's land. Subject to limited exceptions, no new rentcharge can be created after the coming into force of the **Rentcharges Act 1977**. "Estate rentcharges" (those that are attached to freehold land in order to ensure that the burden of positive covenants can bind future purchasers: see Ch.14) are preserved and provide an exception to abolition. Existing rentcharges are to have a maximum life of 60 years calculated from the date of commencement of the rentcharge or the date the Act came into force, whichever is the later.

## Conditions

- although the rentcharge must be "in possession", the **Rentcharges Act 1977** allows rentcharges to be legal even if they are to become payable at a future time after their creation. An exception to the latter rule is where the rentcharge is to take effect following the determination of an earlier interest;
- the rentcharge must be issued out of or charged on land;
- the period of the rentcharge must be fixed or perpetual.

## Charge by Way of Legal Mortgage

Since the **Land Registration Act 2002**, this is the only method by which a legal mortgage can be created in relation to registered land. Previously, as in unregistered land, a mortgage could also be created by the grant of a term of years absolute.

## Rights of Entry

This is a penal right which is employed to enforce forfeiture when a tenant under a legal lease fails to pay rent or to comply with other covenants in the lease. The landlord will usually reserve in the lease a right to re-enter. Similarly, if a legal rentcharge falls into arrears, the grantee has a legal right to enter to collect the money due. The right of entry is a distinct property right.

# OVERREACHING OF TRUST INTERESTS

## Introduction

Overreaching is a process which operates only in relation to co-ownership and only when the purchase money relating to the land is paid to at least two trustees or a trust corporation. In these circumstances, the beneficial interest of the co-owner ceases to be one in the land and becomes transferred into the proceeds of sale. Only certain family interests are capable of being overreached and these are those existing under a strict settlement within the **Settled Land Act 1925** and, most commonly, a beneficial interest under a trust of land.

### Section 2 of the Law of Property Act 1925

This contains the overreaching machinery which applies equally to unregistered and registered land: *City of London Building Society v Flegg* (1988). This is a mechanism which allows the purchaser to take free of a beneficiary's interest (even if the purchaser knows of that interest) provided that the purchase money is paid to at least two trustees or a trust corporation. The latter includes

the Public Trustee, a trustee in bankruptcy and a court appointed trustee corporation. The beneficiary must then look to the trustees for financial recompense.

### Illustrative Cases

- *Williams & Glynns Bank v Boland* (1981) where a wife's beneficial interest
  in land was not overreached because the mortgage money was paid by
  the Bank only to the husband and not, as necessary, to two trustees. This
  ensured that the rights of the wife (as beneficial owner) bound the purchaser Bank.
- *City of London Building Society v Flegg* (1988) where there was an arrangement under which the beneficial interests in a house was shared by
  parents and their adult children. The legal estate was vested in the names
  of the children who proceeded to mortgage the property to the Building
  Society. The interests of the parents had been overreached because the
  mortgage money had been paid to the two legal owners.

### Revision Checklist

You should now know and understand:

- **the basic changes brought about by the 1925 legislation;**
- **the legal estates that may now exist;**
- **the legal interests that may now exist;**
- **the formalities for the creation of legal estates and interests;**
- **the machinery of overreaching.**

## QUESTION AND ANSWER

### Question

Phil is the freeholder of Keele House. Phil has recently engaged in the
following transactions:

i)   he purported to grant a four-year lease of Keele House to Mary
     which is to commence next year. Phil and Mary typed out a draft
     lease and both signed the document;
ii)  Phil orally gave his neighbour Jenny a right to cross Keele House
     as a shortcut to the nearby village;

iii) Phil gave a restrictive covenant by deed, in favour Sally, that he would never build on the extensive gardens of Keele House;

iv) Phil sold a life interest in Keele House to Rosemary.

Advise Phil as to whether he has created any legal interests over the land and whether Rosemary has a legal estate in the land.

## Advice and the Answer

i) This is a reversionary lease in that it is designed to commence at a future date. This can, however, still be a legal lease (estate) for the purposes of s.1(1) of the **Law of Property Act 1925**. There is no requirement that the leasehold estate be in possession (c/f a legal freehold estate). The problem is with the manner of its creation. Section 52 of the **Law of Property Act 1925** imposes the general requirement that a legal estate or interest must be created by deed. An exception to this is contained in s.54(2) and applies to leases. The problem is, however, that the exception applies only to leases not exceeding three years. Mary's lease is for four years and, therefore, falls outside this provision. Hence, Mary does not have a legal estate and (unless it is viewed as a contract to create a legal lease: see Ch. 8) she must be content with an equitable estate in Keele House.

ii) As to Jenny's claim, she would like to assert an easement. Easements are listed in s.1(2) as being capable of existing as a legal interest in land. Obviously, this cannot be a legal easement as there is no deed for the purposes of s.52. In addition, it cannot be an equitable easement because it is not created by writing as required by s.53(1)(a) of the **Law of Property Act 1925**. Hence, it is nothing more than a mere permission to cross Keele House (i.e. it is a bare licence) and is not a property right. Phil can revoke this licence at will.

iii) Phil has entered into a restrictive (i.e. negative) covenant with Sally which is a property right. Although this is created by deed, it is a right not listed in s.1(2) and, therefore, is necessarily an equitable interest (s.1(3)).

iv) A life estate is not listed in s.1(1) as being capable of being a legal estate in land. Hence, Rosemary has acquired merely an equitable estate for life in Keele House. Since 1997, this can exist only behind a trust of land. This means that Phil will hold the legal title subject to the equitable life interest (i.e. beneficial interest) of Rosemary.

# Land Contracts

**5**

........

## INTRODUCTION

In addition to the normal requirements of a contract (e.g. offer and acceptance, an intention to create legal relations and consideration), s.2 of the **Law of Property (Miscellaneous Provisions) Act 1989** provides that for a land contract to be valid it must also be in writing, contain all the express terms and be signed by both parties. The aim of this legislative framework was to simplify the law while instilling certainty and justice into this part of the conveyancing process.

Figure 6

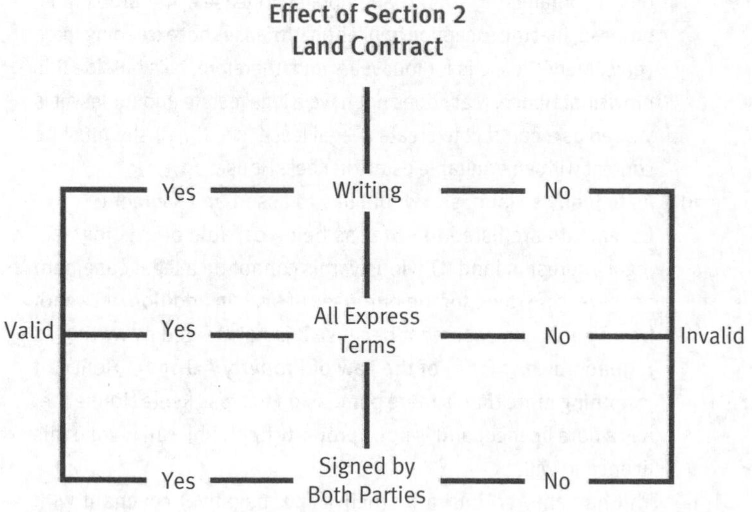

**Effect of Section 2
Land Contract**

........

## EXCEPTIONS

This requirement of signed writing does not, however, apply to short leases (i.e. periodic tenancies and leases which do not exceed three years), contracts (not being a regulated mortgage) under the **Financial Services and Markets Act 2000** and public auction contracts. Similarly, s.2 does not apply to chattel contracts, contracts that have already been performed, collateral contracts, a contract to compulsory purchase property and so-called lock out agreements which prevent negotiation with other prospective purchasers for a specified period. It was held in *Joyce v Rigolli* (2004) that the provision does not cover trivial dispositions of land following an informal boundary agreement between neighbours. In addition, it does not apply to an agreement (e.g. to grant a lease) which is part of a wider composite transaction: *Dolphin Quays Development v Mills* (2006).

## CONTRACTS WITHIN SECTION 2

- the creation of an option to purchase, but not its unilateral exercise (*Spiro v Glencrown Properties Ltd* (1991)) The same applies to the creation and exercise of a right of first refusal: *Bircham & Co Nominees Ltd v Worrell Holdings Ltd* (2001);
- an option to surrender a lease (*Commission for the New Towns v Cooper* (Great Britain) Ltd (1995));
- the creation of a legal or equitable mortgage (*United Bank of Kuwait v Sahib* (1996)); and
- the variation of an existing land contract (*McCausland v Duncan Lawrie* (1996)).

## REQUIREMENTS OF SECTION 2

### Contract
There has to be an agreement to deal with land or an interest in land. Both parties must, therefore, intend to enter into the transaction (i.e. bilateral obligations must be undertaken). In *Ruddick v Ormston* (2005), there was alleged to be a contract written out over two pages in a diary. One page acknowledged that the property was to be sold by the defendant. The other page acknowledged that property was to be bought by the claimant. Although both parties signed both pages, the High Court held that there was no contract at all because neither page set out the mutual obligations of the parties. Note also the effect of the subject to contract label below.

### Writing
This is defined widely by the Interpretation Act 1978 and includes typing, printing, photography, lithography and other modes of representing or reproducing words in a visible form.

### Signature
This is also widely defined and includes any visible mark made by the contracting parties or their authorised agents which is intended to authenticate and

adopt the document: *First Post Homes Ltd v Johnson* (1995). A forged signature would not suffice: *Grunhut v Ramdas* (2002). The signature of an authorised agent will, however, be effective.

### Document

This can include more than one page or piece of paper and it is possible for two documents to be joined together by express or implied reference to one another: *Courtney v Corp Ltd* (2006). Provided that there is this joinder of documents (also known as incorporation of terms), some of the terms can, therefore, be in one document while the remainder are in another: *British Bakeries Ltd v Thorbourne Retail Parks* (1991).

### Exchange of Contracts

This is common in practice and (when the contract is drafted in two identical parts) the contract becomes binding only when both signed parts of the contract have been exchanged.

### Express Terms

These must be stipulated in the written document whereas implied terms (of which there are few) need not be specified. Examples of implied terms are that vacant possession will be given and that conveyance of the property (i.e. completion) will occur within a reasonable time after contract.

### Subject to Contract

This is a label which, when attached to a document, prevents a contract from arising, prevents one document being joined to another and, even though there might be detrimental reliance, operates as a bar to an estoppel claim: *James v Evans* (2000). The label once attached persists until abandoned either expressly or though implication.

## INVALIDITY

### General Rule

Section 2 makes it clear that a contract which does not comply with the formalities is void (i.e. of no effect). It is not merely unenforceable and it has no legal significance whatsoever: *Spiro v Glencrown Properties Ltd* (1991).

### Departures from the General Rule

The outcome of invalidity may be sidestepped in several ways.

## Rectification

This is an equitable remedy by which the court may rectify (i.e. rewrite) the written contract so as to cater for an express term that was agreed, but was by mistake omitted from the written contract. The remedy is recognised in s.2(4) of the 1989 Act. In *Wright v Robert Leonard Developments Ltd* (1994), for example, a term as to the sale of furnishings was left out of the written land contract by mistake. The Court of Appeal rectified the contract so as to include the omitted term and cure the defect. In order for there to be rectification there must be:

- an intention of both parties that the omitted term appear in the written contract;
- by mutual mistake (or, in exceptional circumstances, unilateral mistake) the term was not included in the written contract.

## Collateral Contract

This was a possibility upheld in *Record v Bell* (1991) where the parties agreed that the vendor would offer the purchaser a warranty as to the state of the title to be sold. This was omitted from the written land contract. It was held that this term could be hived off and put within a separate contract outside s.2, collateral to the land contract. The consideration for entering into this collateral contract is provided by the entry into the main contract. As this is a pure fiction (i.e. the parties never intended that there be two contracts), it is a device that the courts appear reluctant to employ.

## Proprietary Estoppel

Although estoppel is not mentioned in the 1989 Act, the court is able at times to invoke an estoppel so as to avoid an unjust outcome. In the context of land contracts, estoppel can be utilised to estop/prevent the other party from relying upon his strict legal rights (i.e. claiming invalidity under s.2 due to an omitted term or, more controversially, the absence of any writing).

## Ingredients

There were three main elements to proprietary estoppel identified by the House of Lords in *Thorner v Major* (2009):

- a representation or assurance made to the claimant which is clear and unequivocal. This requires an inducement to act;
- reliance by the claimant on the representation or assurance which is reasonable in all the circumstances. This requires a causal link between the inducement and the reliance;

- detriment (e.g. the payment of money) incurred as a result of that reliance which is sufficiently substantial to justify the intervention of equity. This requires that it be unjust or inequitable to allow the representation or assurance to be disregarded (this is commonly known as the test of "unconscionabilty"). As Lord Walker put it in *Yeoman's Row Management Ltd v Cobbe* (2008), the result must, "shock the conscience of the court".

## Satisfying the equity

In *Gillett v Holt* (2001), the Court of Appeal advocated what may be called the "minimum equity" test. This entails that the court will make an award to the claimant which marks the minimum required to do justice between the parties. This does not mean that the court should ignore what was assured or expected, it means that the court should look at matters in the round and take on board any benefits that the claimant may have received. For example, in *Jennings v Rice* (2003) the claimant was assured that he would inherit a valuable property if he acted as a full-time residential carer for the owner. The claimant was able to establish an estoppel, but was not awarded the house. Instead, he obtained a financial charge on the house. In promoting the minimum equity approach, the court took into account the benefits he had received over the years (e.g. free board and food). As Aldous L.J. put it, "there must be proportionality between the expectation and the detriment".

## Constructive Trust

As mentioned above, there is some controversy as to whether proprietary estoppel can be employed where the land contract is purely oral. Lord Scott in *Yeoman's Row Management Ltd v Cobbe* (2008) was of the view that estoppel could never be used in these circumstances. Fortunately, for the claimant there is an alternative equitable device which can most certainly operate in relation to oral contracts, i.e. the constructive trust.

## Ingredients

The key features underpinning a constructive trust (which is a device recognised in s.2(5)) are outwardly similar to estoppel:

- there must be an express agreement, arrangement or understanding between the parties (i.e. a common intention);
- the claimant must change his position detrimentally as a result of the understanding (i.e. this would make it unconscionable for the other party to renege on the agreement);
- the court will give effect to an express understanding by enforcing what was agreed (i.e. the failed contract).

*Illustrative case*

In *Yaxley v Gotts* (2000), Mr Yaxley orally agreed with the Mr Gotts that he would redevelop a property into a block of flats. In return, Mr Yaxley was to take the ground floor of the property for himself. The work was carried out, but the parties argued and Mr Yaxley was excluded from the premises. The Court of Appeal declined to invoke a proprietary estoppel, but instead preferred to identify a constructive trust. This enabled the court to order the performance of the trust which arose from the invalid contract.

## Revision Checklist

You should now know and understand:

- **the formalities introduced by s.2 of the 1989 Act;**

- **the types of contract to which it applies and those to which it does not;**

- **the consequence of a non-compliance with s.2;**

- **the scope for rectification, proprietary estoppel and constructive trusts.**

## QUESTION AND ANSWER

### Question

Leonardo is the freeholder of the Turtle Pizza House. He is approached by Raphael who wishes to purchase the restaurant. They orally agree a price and put the matter in the hands of their respective solicitors. Unknown to the solicitors, both parties have agreed that Leonardo will include all the tables and chairs in the purchase price. The solicitors draft the contracts in identical terms, but do not include the term as to the tables and chairs. Following the payment of a 10 per cent deposit by Raphael, signed contracts are subsequently exchanged. Leonardo then telephones Raphael and tells him where he can buy stock and other items for the restaurant. Raphael enters into a series of contracts with the recommended suppliers. Leonardo now wishes to sell the restaurant to a higher bidder and argues that the contract is invalid because of a non-compliance with s.2 of the Law of Property (Miscellaneous Provisions) Act 1989.

   Advise Raphael.

On the facts, there are clearly present all the general ingredients for a binding contract: offer, acceptance, consideration and an absence of vitiating factors. The problem lies with the additional formalities as required by s.2(1). The sale of the restaurant is clearly a land contract and does not fall within one of the exceptions listed in s.2(5). Hence, the contract is caught squarely by the 1989 Act. The requirements of s.2 must, therefore, be analysed.

First, s.2 requires that the contract be in writing. In this case, the parties' respective solicitors write out the contract in two identical parts. It is to be appreciated that the parties intend the contract to become binding only on exchange of contracts and not before. Exchange has duly occurred on the present facts.

Secondly, the written document must incorporate all the express terms agreed between the parties. This is problematic because the term as to tables and chairs is not set out in the written document. These are not fixtures and are not deemed by law to be automatically included in the contract. There are no other documents which can be incorporated by virtue of s.2(2) into the contract in order to cure the defect. Hence, following cases such as *Spiro v Glencrown*, the entire contract is prima facie invalid.

Thirdly, the contract must be signed by both parties or their agents. As exchange of contracts was intended, it suffices that each party signs their respective part of the contract (s.2(3)). This is what will have occurred on the present facts.

In order to save the transaction, Raphael has several alternative arguments:

i) he could argue that both parties intended that the omitted term appear in the written contract and that it was omitted due to a common mistake. Hence, he could invite the court to rectify the agreement to represent the true bargain. The difficulty here is that the parties did not intend the term to appear in the written agreement. If they had so intended they would have informed their respective advisers. Hence, it appears that rectification is unavailable: *Wright v Robert Leonard Developments Ltd*;

ii) following *Record v Bell*, Raphael could argue for a collateral contract separate from the land contract and, therefore, outside s.2. If this was successful, then both contracts could be enforced by Raphael. As mentioned, however, the courts are highly reluctant to sidestep s.2 in such a blatant fashion;

iii) due to the change of position (i.e. entry into the contracts with suppliers) resulting from the assurance that Raphael would be purchasing the restaurant, it could strongly be argued that a proprietary estoppel would arise. All the ingredients appear to be present: assurance, reliance and detriment. Hence, and even though estoppel is not mentioned in s.2(5), Leonardo could be estopped from relying on the omitted term as a means of vitiating the agreement between them: *Thorner v Major*. The payment of a 10 per cent deposit alone is thought not to be sufficient to activate an estoppel. The money can simply be paid back. If that is not possible, then an estoppel could arise from that source as it would then be unconscionable to allow Leonardo to renege from the agreement. In this instance, the minimum equity which the estoppel would satisfy is likely to be the performance of what was agreed;

iv) arising from the same facts, an implied constructive trust could be imposed. This mechanism is listed expressly in s.2(5). There is an express understanding and there has been a change of position by and to the detriment of Raphael: *Yaxley v Gotts*. The court should, therefore, enforce the trust (i.e. the agreement between Raphael and Leonardo).

# Land Charges

**6**

## INTRODUCTION

There are five registers created under the **Land Charges Act 1925** (now 1972), all kept on a central computer at the Land Charges Department of the Land Registry at Plymouth. The five registers are:

- the register of pending actions, which records the existence of disputed claims and litigation affecting the land;
- the register of annuities, which only documents annuities created pre-1926 and is to be closed once all annuitants have died;
- the register of writs and orders affecting land, which discloses charging and bankruptcy orders and the appointment of a receiver;
- the register of deeds of arrangement, which reveals any written arrangements made between the insolvent estate owner and his creditors; and
- the land charges register. It is with this register that the remainder of this chapter is concerned.

## LAND CHARGES ACT 1972

Land charges only concern land where the title to that land is unregistered. If the title is registered, the land is instead subject to very different provisions of the **Land Registration Act 2002** (see Ch.7). The **Land Charges Act 1972** enables the registration of a land charge to protect some (but not all) third party interests in land. Those interests that are outside the scheme remain subject to the doctrine of notice (see Ch.3) and, as regards an interest under a trust or settlement, the overreaching machinery (see below). Otherwise, the system of land charges has supplanted the doctrine of notice in respect of third party rights in unregistered land. Persons dealing with unregistered land are expected to make a search of the land charges register against the names of previous owners in order to discover any protected interests.

## Principles of Land Charges Registration
### *Is the interest registrable?*

After 1925, if a third party right is registrable (i.e. there is a class of land charge specifically tailored to protect it) its potential to bind a future purchaser of the land depends upon whether or not an appropriate land charge has been validly registered.

### *If it is registered?*

Registration of a land charge is deemed to constitute actual notice to all persons and for all purposes connected with the land: s.198 of the **LPA 1925**. Registration of a land charge will ensure that the interest binds a new purchaser. The right, therefore, becomes inescapable.

### *If it is not registered?*

A failure to protect a registrable interest by the entry of land charge will, as a general rule, make the interest void against a purchaser for value of any interest in the land: s.4 of the **LCA 1972**. Where, however, the interest is of a commercial nature (as opposed to a family interest) a different approach may be discerned. This difference of treatment concerns either an estate contract (Civ); a charge in relation to unpaid inheritance tax (Di); restrictive covenant (Dii); or equitable easement (Diii). These interests will only be void for non-registration against a purchaser of a legal estate who gives money or money's worth. Whether a purchaser has actual notice or not in these situations is irrelevant: s.199(1) of the **LPA**. The limited exception to this rule is when to rely upon the non-registration would amount to a fraud: *Midland Bank v Green* (1981).

## Name of the Estate Owner

Land charges are registered against the name of the estate owner at the time the interest is created, not against the land. The working rule is that the correct name is that as specified in the title deeds. The fact that names will get lost in the mists of time, moreover, is a major defect of the land charges scheme. An official search of the land charges register will be conclusive if made against the correct names of the estate owners and it provides 15 working days immunity against any subsequent entries. Obvious problems can arise where an incorrect version of the name is used either to register a charge or to make a search of the register.

*Illustrative cases*

- In *Oak Co-operative Building Society v Blackburn* (1968) a land charge was entered against the name of Frank David Blackburn. A search of the land charges register was made against the name of Francis Davis Blackburn. The correct name, however, was Francis David Blackburn so both the registration and the search were made against the wrong names. Faced with this dilemma, the court took the view that a land charge registered against a version of the correct name was valid against someone who searched against an incorrect version.
- In *Diligent Finance Ltd v Alleyne* (1972) a class F land charge was registered by Mrs Alleyne against the name of Erskine Alleyne. The estate owner's correct name was, however, Erskine Owen Alleyne. The land charge was held to be void against a purchaser who searched against the correct name.

## Categories of Land Charge

Within the land charges register there are six classifications (classes A–F) of land charge, although only classes C, D and F require much attention here. The other less significant classes are:

- class A which caters for money charged on land indirectly imposed by statute (e.g. a landlord's right to compensation under the Agricultural Holdings Act 1986);
- class B which deals with charges on land directly imposed by Parliament (e.g. the Legal Services Commission charge on land in respect of property recovered or preserved by a "legally aided" individual imposed by the Access to Justice Act 1999); and
- class E which embraces annuities created before 1926 which are not registered in the register of annuities.

### Class C land charges

C(i) protects a puisne (pronounced "puny") mortgage, that is, a legal mortgage not protected by deposit of title deeds. The possession of title deeds offers ultimate protection and first priority for a lender: s.97 of the **LPA 1925**.

C(ii) protects a limited owner's charge, that is, a financial charge on the land entered by a person who is not an absolute owner. For example, a tenant for life who pays inheritance tax out of his own pocket may protect payment in this way.

C(iii) protects a general equitable charge which is not protected by title deeds. This extends to an equitable, financial charge which is not registrable under any other class, for example, an equitable mortgage, an unpaid vendor's lien, and an equitable rentcharge.

C(iv) protects a contract to convey or create a legal estate. The contract must amount to a binding and enforceable agreement which means that it must satisfy the writing formalities of s.2 of the **Law of Property (Miscellaneous Provisions) Act 1989**. The definition covers ordinary contracts for sale, leasing or mortgaging of the legal estate, as well as a right of pre-emption (first refusal) and an option to purchase. A request for an overriding lease under s.20(6) of the Landlord and Tenant (Covenants) Act 1995 (see Ch.15) may also be registered as a C(iv) land charge.

### Class D land charges

D(i) can be entered by the Inland Revenue in respect of unpaid inheritance tax in respect of land.

D(ii) protects a restrictive covenant provided that it was entered into after 1925 and was not made between a landlord and tenant. Restrictive covenants made prior to 1926 are still governed by the doctrine of notice. Leasehold covenants are governed by very different rules (see Ch.15).

D(iii) protects an equitable easement that was created after 1925. Rights acquired by estoppel are not within this category and are not registrable: *Ives v High* (1967). Pre-1926 equitable easements remain governed by the doctrine of notice.

### Class F land charge

The class F land charge caters for the protection of the right of occupation given to spouses by the **Family Law Act 1996**. This right is extended also to same sex registered partners under s.101 of the **Civil Partnership Act 2004**. If, for example, a husband holds the legal estate as sole owner or on trust for himself and his wife by way of co-ownership, the wife will have the right to register a charge and protect her rights of occupation: see *Wroth v Tyler* (1974). The entry of a class F land charge can be made without the consent of the owning spouse. If the process is misused by a spouse, the court has the power to cancel the land charge: *Barnett v Hassett* (1981).

## Interests Outside the Scheme
### Legal interests

With the exception of puisne mortgages (C(i)), legal interests fall outside the land charges machinery and, therefore, remain automatically binding in rem on all the world.

*Equitable interests*

Some equitable interests are also outside the scheme and whether they will bind a purchaser will depend upon the doctrine of notice. Such interests include:

- restrictive covenants and equitable easements created before 1926;
- beneficial interests under a trust of land (such interests can, however, be overreached: see below);
- equitable rights of entry; and
- equitable rights based on estoppel.

Figure 7

## Property Rights in Unregistered Land

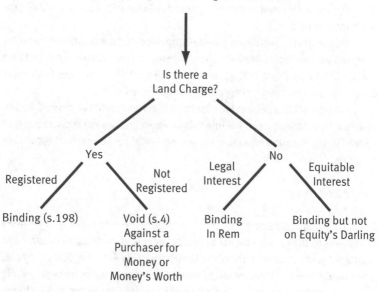

## THE LAW OF PROPERTY ACT 1969

### Hidden Names

On investigating title, it is possible that the name of a previous estate owner, against whom a land charge has been entered, is not disclosed. It may be hidden behind the (minimum of 15 years) root of title. Nevertheless, the purchaser will be bound by such an undiscoverable land charge. The problem was partly addressed in s.25 of the 1969 Act which allows for such a purchaser to claim compensation from the public purse. This is, of course, provided that he did not actually know of the land charge.

## Discovery After Contract

It is usual for a land charges search to be made only after contracts have been entered, but before completion of the transaction. A land charge discovered after contract remains binding, but s.24 of the 1969 Act allows the purchaser to withdraw from the contract. This is again provided that the purchaser did not actually know of the land charge.

### Revision Checklist

You should now know and understand:

- which interests in land can be protected by the entry of a land charge;

- the consequences flowing from the registration of land charge;

- the consequences flowing from non-registration;

- the effect of the Law of Property Act 1969.

## QUESTION AND ANSWER

### Question

Some years ago, Jane purchased Tay House (the title to which is unregistered) from Gill. Subsequently, a variety of claims were made against the property on the basis of the following encumbrances:

i)    a claim by Gill to a restrictive covenant which was granted in the conveyance to Jane;

ii)   a claim by Ron to an easement;

iii)  a claim by Maurice (Gill's estranged husband) to a statutory right of occupation;

iv)   an undischarged mortgage entered between between Gill and the Easy Credit Co.

Outlining what further information (if any) you may require, advise Jane.

The key point here is that this problem question is to do with unregistered land, land charges and the residual role of the doctrine of notice. The answer must address the different types of property right mentioned and elicit information such as to whether any given right amounts to a legal or equitable interest, whether there is a land charge available, whether a land charge has been registered and whether, if the right falls outside the statutory scheme, Jane has notice of it.

i)  a restrictive covenant is not listed in s.1(2) of the **Law of Property Act 1925** and, therefore, must always be an equitable interest in land. For the purposes of the **Land Charges Act 1972**, a restrictive covenant may be protected by the entry of a Dii land charge. This applies only to freehold negative covenants (as here) which were created after 1925. Information is needed as to when this covenant was created. If it is pre-1926, then the doctrine of notice will apply. Hence, the covenant will bind Jane unless she is a bona fide purchaser for value of the legal estate without notice (i.e. "Equity's Darling"). She clearly satisfies the majority of these conditions and there is no reason to doubt her bona fides. The issue would, therefore, turn upon whether she had actual, constructive or imputed notice of the covenant. If so, she will be bound by it. If not, she will take free of it. If the covenant was created after 1925, the focus is upon whether a Dii land charge was registered. If it was, then the covenant will bind Gill (s.198 of the **LPA 1925**) because it is deemed to constitute actual notice to the world. If it was not registered, it will be void for non-registration by virtue of s.4 of the **LCA 1972** against a purchaser for money or money's worth (i.e. Jane);

ii)  an easement is listed in s.1(2) of the 1925 Act and can, therefore, be a legal interest in land. All depends upon how it was created: if it was created by deed then it will be a legal easement and, if it was not, then it must necessarily be equitable (s.52 of the **LPA 1925**). Accordingly, it is important to know whether this is a legal or equitable easement. If it is legal, there is no land charge available and the right falls outside the **Land Charges Act**. Hence, as it is a legal interest it binds Jane and everyone else automatically (i.e. it binds in rem). If it is not a legal easement, there is a land charge which protects certain types of equitable easement (i.e. the Diii land charge). This extends only to those equitable easements created after 1925. It is necessary, therefore, to ascertain when this easement was created. If it is pre-1926, then (as discussed in connection with the restrictive covenant) it will depend upon whether Jane is "Equity's Darling" and, in particular, whether she had notice of the easement. If it is post-1925, it all depends whether a Diii land charge was entered. If so, it will bind Jane, but if not it will be void against her for non-registration;

iii) as to the statutory right of occupation which arises under the **Family Law Act 1996**, this is an equitable interest and a Class F land charge can be entered unilaterally by Maurice. If so, it will bind Jane by virtue of s.198 of the 1925 Act. If the land charge is not registered, it will be void against a purchaser for value under s.4 of the 1972 Act. If a Class F land charge has been used by Maurice for no gain other than to spite his wife (as in *Wroth v Tyler*), the court now has the ability to cancel the land charge: *Barnett v Hassett*;

iv) in relation to the undischarged mortgage, much turns on the nature of the mortgage itself. If it is legal or equitable and protected by title deeds (which it appears is not the case here as Jane has purchased the property), then it will bind a purchaser automatically. The holding of the title deeds offers sufficient protection. If it is legal and not protected by title deeds (a possibility here) there is a Ci land charge which can be entered to protect such a "puisne" mortgage. If registered, it will bind. If not, it will be void for non-registration against a purchaser for money or money's worth (i.e. Jane). In the case where the mortgage is equitable and not protected by title deeds, a Ciii land charge is available. Again, if it is registered it will bind Jane (s.198 **LPA 1925**) and if not it will be void against her for non-registration (s.4 of the **LCA 1972**).

# Registered Land

## 7

## INTRODUCTION

The object of registration of title is to make the transfer of land simpler, quicker, cheaper and more reliable. The ambition of registered conveyancing is to do away with the onerous requirement of repeated examination of title deeds on successive sales. In its place, there is a three part register which provides for the purchaser a description of the land, the name of the registered proprietor and any third party rights which are registered against the land. In this way, the purchaser should have a complete and up-to-date picture of the state of the title which, if accompanied by enquiries of the vendor and a physical inspection of the land, should provide adequate protection. The system, however, is not perfect in that certain rights override a registered disposition and are binding upon a purchaser even though they are not recorded on the register. The registered system has recently undergone major overhaul in the form of the **Land Registration Act 2002** (in force since October 13, 2003). This repeals the **Land Registration Act 1925** in its entirety. The changes introduced are radical and, unfortunately, complex.

### Phasing Out Unregistered Land

The system of registered conveyancing is rapidly subsuming its unregistered counterpart and, since 1990, the whole of England and Wales has been an area of compulsory registration. Around 90 per cent of titles in England and Wales are now registered. This means that on the next sale or other disposition of unregistered land the title will have to be registered, i.e. compulsory first registration will take place. The events that trigger this first registration are considered below.

> **AIMS**
> The **Land Registration Act 2002** is designed to achieve a variety of purposes. The major ones are:
>
> - to make all titles to land registered by extending the range of events which trigger compulsory first registration and allowing Crown land to be registered;

- to pave the way for electronic conveyancing (e-conveyancing) and to make the land register capable of easy online investigation. Registration will then take place simultaneously with the creation of estates and interests and, thereby, the current registration gap of two months will disappear;
- to provide more effective protection for title to land and third party rights;
- to ensure that the register is an accurate reflection of title by reducing the categories of overriding interest;
- to ensure that most express dispositions of land are noted on the register; and
- to introduce a new system of acquiring title by adverse possession.

## BASIC PRINCIPLES OF REGISTERED CONVEYANCING

It is often said that there are three fundamental principles underpinning the system of registered title.

### The Mirror Principle

This entails or requires that the register should be an accurate reflection of the current title and matters affecting the land. The 2002 Act has heightened the reflective nature of the register by reducing the number of rights that exist off-register and increasing the number of rights that must be protected on the register in order to bind third parties. The aim is that title to land can be investigated with the bare minimum of additional enquiries. A major crack in this mirror principle concerns overriding interests (now styled "interests which override either first registration or registered dispositions") which do not appear on the register, but are automatically binding on a purchaser. The major unregistered interests that override are considered below.

### The Curtain Principle

This operates to hide any interest arising under a trust behind the curtain of registration. This means that interests that can be overreached by a purchaser (by paying the purchase money to two trustees or a trust corporation) are not detailed on the register. Instead, the existence of a trust interest might be disclosed by the entry by a beneficiary of a restriction on the Land Register. This will alert a purchaser that there is a trust interest that must be overreached. A beneficial interest cannot be protected by the entry of a notice (s.33(a)).

### The Insurance Principle

This relates to the state guarantee as to the accuracy of title as declared on the register. The state will pay compensation to any person who suffers loss as a result of an error or inaccuracy on the face of the register: s.58 of the **LRA 2002**. Rectification and alteration of any errors on the register is, however, possible: s.65 (see below).

## THE LAND REGISTER

### Background

Section 1 of the 2002 Act provides that a register of title is to be maintained by the Land Registry. The Land Registry is headed by the Chief Land Registrar. Applications for registration are dealt with by district land registries and each has its own regional catchment area. The system is computerised. Since 1988, the Land Register has been open to public inspection which means that anyone, on the payment of the appropriate fee, may obtain a print out of an individual register of title. The register of title for individual properties is structured in three parts.

### The Property Register

This contains a geographical description of the land with reference to a plan. A legal description of the property is also included and this will note the advantageous features of the land such as any easements and restrictive covenants which exist for the benefit of the land. If the title is leasehold, details of the lease will be provided here.

### The Proprietorship Register

This specifies the class of title that has been registered, the name and address of the proprietor and any restrictions entered which limit the ability of the registered proprietor to deal with the land.

### The Charges Register

This contains entries of third party rights burdening the land, e.g. mortgages, estoppel rights, land contracts, equitable easements and restrictive covenants.

## WHAT CAN BE REGISTERED?

### Rights Capable of Substantive Registration

Only a very limited number of estates and interests can be substantively registered and this means that these rights can be registered with their own separate title and, thereby, each is given its own unique title number. A failure to register will mean that legal title will not pass. A list of these rights is contained in s.2 of the **LRA 2002**. They include a fee simple absolute in possession (freehold), a term of years absolute exceeding seven years' duration (leasehold), a profit a prendre existing in gross (i.e. without there being a dominant tenement), a rentcharge and a franchise (a royal privilege). The person registered is known as the "registered proprietor".

## Rights Capable of Non-Substantive Registration

There are even fewer rights which are capable of non-substantive registration. The two major examples of this are legal mortgages and express legal easements.

### Legal mortgage of registered land

This must be created by a charge expressed to be by way of legal mortgage (s.23(1)(a)). The charge must then be registered by the lender in the charges register relating to the mortgaged land and then becomes known as a registered charge. It is only on registration that the mortgage takes effect as a legal charge: s.51. Mortgagees no longer obtain a charge certificate following registration. Registration now provides the protection for a mortgage lender.

### Legal easements

Legal easements that have been expressly created require a notice to be entered on the charges register of the title to the burdened land (i.e. the servient tenement). It is also a requirement that the benefit be registered in the property register of the title to the benefited land (i.e. the dominant tenement) which makes the grantee the proprietor of the legal easement or profit. Until the registration process is complete, the easement remains equitable. Registration, therefore, completes the process of creating an express legal easement or legal profit.

## Registrable Interests

Other types of rights are called registrable interests. Such interests must be protected by the agreed or unilateral entry of a notice in the charges register (s.34(2)). Unilateral notices are appropriate where the registered proprietor does not agree to the entry. On entry of the unilateral notice, the Registrar will notify the registered proprietor and the latter can then apply for the notice to be cancelled. The matter can, if necessary, be referred to an adjudicator appointed under the 2002 Act. Interests which are to be protected by a notice are traditionally known as minor interests and include most property rights, for example, leases granted for more than three years, equitable easements, restrictive covenants, estate contracts, spousal rights of occupation, rights or pre-emption and estoppel rights.

### Some observations

- the general rule is that, if protected by a notice, the interest will bind a purchaser (s.29(2) of the **LRA 2002**) whereas, if it is not, it will be void for non-registration against a new registered proprietor (s.29(1));
- a number of rights cannot, however, be protected by a notice and these include a beneficial interest under a trust of land or Settled Land Act trust, leasehold covenants and leases which were granted for three years or less: s.33 ((a)–(c));
- if the claimant is in actual occupation, however, unregistered or unregistrable rights might be binding as an interest that overrides registration (i.e. an overriding interest); and
- remember that the doctrine of notice (as considered in Ch. 3) has no application to registered land.

## Illustrations: Leases, Easements and Mortgages
### Leases

- a legal lease over seven years in duration must be substantively registered with its own title number. If not it is regarded as a contract to create a legal lease and remains equitable;
- a legal lease of seven years or less cannot be substantively registered, but may fall within its own category of overriding interest and will then bind a purchaser;
- a legal or equitable lease of three years and more may be protected by the entry of a notice on the Charges Register; and
- a legal or equitable lease of less than three years cannot be protected by a notice nor can it be an overriding interest in its own right. If the tenant is in actual occupation, however, it can fall within the class of overriding interest that deals with actual occupation.

### Easements

- an express legal easement must be non-substantively registered, i.e. the burden must be protected by the entry of a notice on the title of the burdened land and the benefit must be registered on the title of the benefited land. Until this occurs, the easement is equitable in nature;
- an implied legal easement potentially falls within its own class of overriding interest; and

- an equitable easement must be protected by the entry of a notice on the charges register.

### Mortgages

- a legal mortgage can, following the **Land Registration Act 2002**, only be made by legal charge. Once a legal charge is executed, it has to be entered on the Charges Register relating to the land. It is then called a registered charge. The date of registration of the charge will be stated on the register. As to priority between registered charges, the rule is that the mortgages rank in the order in which they are entered on the Land Register. This is irrespective of the order of their creation;
- an equitable mortgage may be protected by entry of a notice on the Charges Register relating to the land. If so, it will take priority over a later mortgage whether that is a registered charge or an interest which is protected by notice on the Charges Register.

## REGISTERED ESTATES

### Introduction
When land is first registered, the nature of the title described in the proprietorship register will depend upon the proof of the title that the estate owner can demonstrate. The guarantee afforded will reflect the type of title that is registered and might also differ according to whether the title is freehold or leasehold.

### Absolute Title
This applies to both freehold and leasehold estates, is the best and most common title available. It is registered only when the Registrar can verify that the title is safe and cannot be significantly challenged. In the case of freehold land, s.11 provides that the proprietor registered with absolute title takes subject only to incumbrances and other entries on the register and overriding interests (unless the contrary is stated on the register). In the case of leasehold land, s.12 ensures that registration with absolute title guarantees to the world that the lease was validly granted (i.e. that superior titles have been investigated and that the landlord had the capacity to grant the lease). This, however, the Registrar is not always able to do.

### Good Leasehold Title
This, not surprisingly, applies only to a leasehold estate and has no relevance to freeholds: s.10. This title is appropriate where the landlord's title has not yet been registered. Otherwise, it is the same as absolute title: s.12(6).

## Qualified Title

This is relevant in those rare situations where there is a defect in, or doubt as to, title which prevents registration with absolute title. For example, title might have been acquired in breach of trust or when, on first registration, title has been established only for a limited period. Qualified title extends to both freehold and leasehold land (ss.9 and 10) and is similar to absolute title except that it is subject to the potential defect.

## Possessory Title

This is applied for when, on first registration, the applicant is unable to produce any title deeds. This arises where the claim to freehold or leasehold title is based upon adverse possession (squatter's rights). Possessory title is rare, but has the same effect as absolute title except that it does not affect or prejudice the enforcement of any other estate or rights which existed at the time of first registration: s.12.

## Upgrading Title

Section 62 permits the Registrar, either of his own volition or at the request of a person interested (usually, the registered proprietor himself), to upgrade title.

- If the title is freehold, either a qualified or possessory title can be upgraded to absolute title.
- In the case of possessory title, this regrading can occur when the title has been registered for 12 years.
- If title is leasehold, a qualified or possessory title can be upgraded to good leasehold title if the Registrar no longer has doubts as to the validity of the lease.
- Any of those leasehold titles can be regraded to absolute title when the Registrar is assured of the title of the landlord (e.g. the freeholder's title has now been registered in its own right).

## Failure to Register

Section 6 imposes a duty to register on the transferee of a relevant estate. An application to register a freehold or leasehold title, moreover, must be made within two months of either a registered disposition or a triggering event: s.6(4). This period can be extended by the Registrar if there is good cause to do so. If registration has not been applied for within this time frame, the transaction is void as to legal title and, instead, the existing registered proprietor will usually hold the legal title on trust for the transferee: s.7(2)(a). In relation to a lease/ mortgage, however, the disposition takes effect as a contract to create a legal lease/mortgage (s.7(2)(b)). The danger is that the transferee (particularly a mortgagee) could lose priority to an interest created after the ineffective disposition.

## First Registration

As unregistered land is being rapidly phased out, s.3 of the 2002 Act allows for voluntary first registration of title and encourages this by offering discounted fees. Compulsory/mandatory registration of what was previously legal title in unregistered land is required on the occurrence of certain triggering events. The duty to register and the sanctions of non-registration are as explained above. The transactions which operate to trigger first registration of previously unregistered title are set out in s.4 and include:

- the transfer of a freehold estate or an assignment of a leasehold estate (with seven years of more remaining unexpired). This does not include the surrender of a lease;
- the grant out of qualifying freehold (or leasehold estate) of a lease (or sublease) of more than seven years. This does not include the surrender of a lease;
- the grant by a local authority of a right to buy lease to an existing periodic tenant under the Housing Act 1985;
- the creation of a reversionary tenancy (i.e. a tenancy to take effect in the future) which is to take effect in possession more than three months subsequent to its grant; and
- the creation of a first legal mortgage whether of a freehold or leasehold estate (with more than seven years still to run). Taking out a subsequent second mortgage of unregistered land will not, therefore, trigger mandatory registration.

## Cautions Against First Registration

As an application for first registration may well affect the interests of others, in certain circumstances the 2002 Act allows for those interested to lodge a caution against first registration. The effect of this is that, when the application for first registration is made, the person who entered the caution will be notified and given the opportunity to object to the registration. If such objection is made then, short of agreement, the matter must be referred to the adjudicator: s.71. A person may lodge a caution against first registration when he claims to be either the owner of a qualifying estate or entitled to an interest affecting a qualifying estate (e.g. matters such as a land contract which is registrable under the Land Charges Act 1972). Cautions will be noted in a register of cautions which will be maintained at the Land Registry. A caution must be entered only with reasonable cause and, if not, the landowner can apply for it to be cancelled.

# INTERESTS WHICH OVERRIDE REGISTRATION

## Context

These rights are familiarly known as overriding interests because they bind a purchaser even though they do not appear on the registered title. The scope of rights which may benefit from this special treatment have been dramatically reduced by the **Land Registration Act 2002**. This curtailment is designed to simplify the system and reinforce the mirror principle (see above).

## Rights which Override First Registration

Schedule 1 lists the interests which override first registration (ie. those rights which are deemed to be sufficiently important that they will automatically become binding when unregistered title is converted into registered title). Unlike the interests that override subsequent dealings with registered land (see below), this list is more straightforward. Admittedly, however, some similarities are shared between the two schedules. The list includes:

- leases not exceeding seven years (para.1);
- an interest belonging to a person in actual occupation, except for an interest under a strict settlement (para.2). This is to be contrasted with the much more complex provisions considered in the context of interests which override a subsequent disposition of registered land; and
- a legal easement or profit whether expressly or impliedly granted (para.3). Again this is less complicated than the equivalent provisions which deal with interests that override registered dispositions.

## Rights which Override Registered Dispositions

These are more complicated than those which concern first registration and are set out in Sch.3.

### Legal leases for seven years or less (paragraph 1)

This is designed to cater for short leases. Those leases over seven years fall to be substantively registered with their own titles. Legal leases of over three years, but no more than seven years, can alternatively be protected by the entry of a notice.

### Interests of persons in actual occupation (paragraph 2)

This will protect all property rights of the occupier unless excluded. Hence, it is important to appreciate the types of right that can never fall within the scope of para.2. First, the rights always excluded are strict settlements, spousal rights of occupation given under the **Family Law Act 1996**, overriding leases granted under the **Landlord and Tenant (Covenants) Act 1995** and reversionary leases which are not to commence within three months of their grant. These can never be protected under para.2. Secondly, there are some factual situations where actual occupation will offer no protection:

- the rights of the actual occupier of whom enquiry was made who has failed to disclose the right when he reasonably should have done so (para.2(b));
- cases where occupation was not obvious on a reasonably careful inspection of the land at the time of the disposition (para.2(c)(i)) and not within the actual knowledge of the disponee when the disposition occurred (para.2(c)(ii));
- legal easements or profits a prendre (but not their equitable counterparts) that arise through prescription (i.e. long user) or by implication (e.g. under the rule in *Wheeldon v Burrows* (1879) or by virtue of s.62 of the **Law of Property Act 1925**)

Unless:

(i) as regards an easement created after October 13, 2006, it is within the actual knowledge of the purchaser or it would have been obvious on a reasonably careful inspection of the land over which the easement or profit is exercisable; or

(ii) whenever created, the right has been exercised within the period of one year before the disposition or the right has been registered as a right of common under the **Commons Act 2006**.

**Figure 8**

## Property Rights

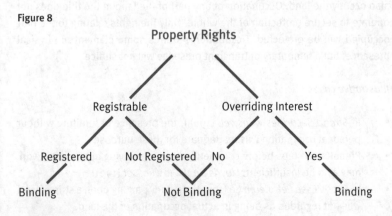

# ACTUAL OCCUPATION

## Context

As shown, the rights of a person in actual occupation may amount to an interest which, although not appearing on the Register, can override a registered disposition. It is, therefore, important to understand the workings of this major incursion upon the mirror principle.

## Actual occupation is the Trigger

This overriding interest protects the rights of persons in actual occupation, not the occupation itself: *National Provincial Bank Ltd v Hastings Car Mart Ltd* (1964). Accordingly, it is necessary to show that there exists a property right that is capable of being protected and that the person claiming it is in actual occupation of the land. The right must subsist in reference to land (i.e. not merely be a personal right such as licence) and must not be excluded by the 2002 Act (see above). Otherwise the rule is that any property right, whether legal or equitable, can be protected by occupation. For example estoppel interests and mere equities (such as arise under *Barclays Bank v O'Brien* (1994) in relation to undue influence and misrepresentation: see Ch. 10) are included. In *Williams & Glyn's Bank Ltd v Boland* (1981), it was held that a wife's beneficial interest under a trust of land could be protected by virtue of her occupation. This, of course, cannot occur if the interest has been overreached: *City of London Building Society v Flegg* (1988). In *Webb v Pollmount Ltd* (1966) an option to purchase the freehold was protected by the fact of occupation by the grantee as tenant.

## Meaning of Actual Occupation

Whether a person is in actual occupation is an issue of fact and the words must be given their ordinary and plain meaning. It does not matter that others may also occupy the land. Occupation of any part of the land in the title does not operate to secure protection of the whole. Only the rights relating to the part occupied will be protected. Occupation requires some element of physical presence, but a temporary or transient presence will not suffice.

### *Illustrative cases*

- In *Strand Securities v Caswell* (1965), the presence of furniture without personal occupation was inadequate for these purposes.
- Preparatory steps before completion such as carrying out building work may also be insufficient: *Lloyds Bank Plc v Rosset* (1991).
- In *Epps v Esso Petroleum Co* (1973), regularly parking upon a strip of land was not regarded as being in actual occupation of the land.

- It is possible to occupy though an agent or member of the family (e.g. a caretaker employed to look after a flat), but a child in occupation of premises is not "in actual occupation" for its parent for the purpose of the section: *Hypo-Mortgage Services Ltd v Robinson* (1997).

### Temporary absences

Temporary absences do not prevent a person being in actual occupation. In *Chhokar v Chhokar* (1984), for example, a wife was in hospital having a baby and yet remained in occupation throughout. Although the husband sold the land and left with the proceeds of sale, the purchaser was still bound by her interest. The duration of the absence and an intention to return appear to be the key factors: *Thompson v Foy* (2009). This theme was reiterated in *Link Lending Ltd v Hussein* (2009), where the county court found there to be actual occupation when at the time of the mortgage the woman was being cared for in an institution, her intention was to return; her furniture and personal effects remained there; she visited the property periodically; no-one else was living there and she paid for regular outgoings in relation to the property.

## Timing of Actual Occupation

The occupation must exist when the transfer to the purchaser takes effect: *Abbey National Building Society v Cann* (1991). Moving into occupation subsequent to this time, but before registration of the purchaser's title, is not sufficient. In *Link Lending Ltd v Hussein* (2009), a voidable transfer was made by a woman who was not mentally able to understand the import of the transaction and who did not remember the transaction having taken place. The transferee mortgaged the property and defaulted on the repayments. The lender sought to take possession and the transferor claimed successfully to be in actual occupation. The county court emphasised that the time she had to be in actual occupation was when the charge was created.

## Consequences

The consequences of having this type of overriding interest will reflect the type of right that is protected by actual occupation and the surrounding circumstances. For example, in *Pritchard Englefield v Steinberg* (2004) a mother had a life interest in her son's flat that arose under a constructive trust. She was in actual occupation and enjoyed an overriding interest that bound subsequent purchasers. The High Court would not allow her to remain in occupation for her life and, instead, ordered that the flat be sold. Her life interest was to be valued and she could claim that amount from the sale proceeds. In *Link Lending Ltd v Hussein* (2009), the lender took subject to the overriding interest and could not, therefore, enforce its charge against the property.

# ALTERATIONS OF THE REGISTER AND INDEMNITY

## Context

Registered title is a state guaranteed title, but even if a proprietor has absolute title there may be situations where, due to error or fraud, the register is inaccurate. For example, the reliability of title offered on first registration may later turn out to be unwarranted or an undisclosed interest affecting the land may subsequently emerge. Schedule 4 of the 2002 Act allows two forms of corrective response.

### Rectification

Rectification of the register can occur in circumstances where there is the correction of a mistake which will prejudicially affect the title of the registered proprietor (para.1). For example, this would occur where a person has wrongly been registered as the proprietor of the land. Where the registered proprietor is in physical possession, the power to rectify is heavily curtailed. No order can be made by the court or the Land Registrar without the registered proprietor's consent unless either he has by fraud or lack of care caused or substantially contributed to the mistake or it would be unjust for rectification not to occur.

### Alteration

Alteration of the register in circumstances where there is no resulting prejudice to the registered proprietor (para.2). As regards to alterations, there is no extra protection afforded to a registered proprietor who is in possession. An order may be obtained either from the court or the Land Registrar for alterations in order:

- to correct a mistake (e.g. where a land charge had not been protected by notice on first registration);
- to bring the register up-to-date (e.g. when an entry was made as a result of fraud);
- to give effect to any right exempted from the effect of registration (e.g. when qualified title is registered and a defect in title is later established); and
- to remove superfluous entries. It is the Registrar (but not the court) who enjoys this latter power to alter the register.

## Indemnity

The payment of an indemnity from the public purse is available under Sch. 8 for loss due to the rectification of the register (e.g. because of forgery or an error in marking of boundaries or mis-stating the length of a lease). This is the practical application of the "insurance principle" underpinning registered conveyancing. This indemnity is not generally available for mere alterations because, as they do not prejudicially affect the registered proprietor, there is technically no loss caused: *Re Chowood* (1933). Indemnity will be denied where the loss arises because of the fraud or lack of care of the claimant (para.5). If the claimant is only partly at fault, indemnity can be scaled down to reflect the degree of culpability (para.5(2)). A six-year limitation period in which to claim indemnity applies (para.8).

## ADVERSE POSSESSION AND REGISTERED LAND

### Meaning
Adverse possession (sometimes called squatter's rights) occurs when an estate owner's rights are extinguished by his failing to evict a trespasser from the land within a prescribed period of time (12 years in unregistered land). The rewards for the squatter can be great. In *Ellis v Lambeth BC* (2000) a squatter, because of his factual possession, obtained title to a house worth £200,000. In *JA Pye (Oxford) Ltd v Graham* (2002), moreover, a squatter acquired title to land worth a staggering £10 million.

### The New Regime
Sections 96–98 and Sch.6 to the **LRA 2002** introduce a new regime for dealing with adverse possession in relation to registered title (obviously the changes do not affect unregistered land). A squatter will now be able to apply to be a registered proprietor with possessory title after 10 years' adverse possession. The onus is, therefore, shifted squarely upon the shoulders of the squatter. The registered proprietor and others interested in the land will be notified of the application. If the application is unopposed within a period of two years, the squatter will become the new registered proprietor of the land.

### *Unsuccessful opposition*

Opposition will usually defeat the claim, but exceptions to this rule include:

- where it would be unconscionable because of an estoppel for the squatter to be dispossessed;
- for some other reason, the squatter is entitled to be registered. For example, in *Bridges v Mees* (1957), the purchaser had paid the full purchase price, but the land was never conveyed to him. He moved into possession and later claimed title by adverse possession; and

- where it is a boundary dispute and the squatter reasonably believed, for at least the 10-year period, that the disputed land was his.

## Revision Checklist

You should now know and understand:

- **the principles underlying the system of registered conveyancing;**
- **the divisions of the Land Register;**
- **the types of title;**
- **those interests which override first registration and a subsequent disposition;**
- **the meaning and effect of actual occupation;**
- **when alterations may be made to the Land Register.**

# QUESTION AND ANSWER

## Question

Norma lives with her husband, John, in Manor House (the title to which is registered). Although Norma has financially contributed towards the purchase of the property, the title is registered in the sole name of John. Last month Norma was rushed to hospital for a serious operation and, while she was away from home, John sold the property to David. John assured David that no-one other than himself resided in the house. Norma is now out of hospital and seeks your advice. John is believed to be living somewhere in South America.

## Advice and the Answer

It is necessary to consider whether (and if so what) property rights Norma has in Manor House. By way of the direct payments made to the purchase price, Norma will have acquired a beneficial interest under a trust of land. The problem question, however, does not provide sufficient detail to assess what share she is likely to have in the property. Her beneficial interest cannot be protected by the entry of a notice on the charges register. It is possible to enter a restriction on the proprietorship register which alerts a purchaser to the existence of a trust and the need to pay the purchase money to two trustees or a trust corporation. It is unlikely that Norma would think of doing this and that, if she had, David would have gone ahead with the purchase. Hence, there is likely to be nothing on the register to make David aware of Norma's trust interest.

The question reveals that the title has already been registered. Hence, there is no need to consider interests which override first registration. The sale to David is a registered disposition and within Sch. 3 of the **Land Registration Act 2002**. Paragraph 2 deals with the interests of a person in actual occupation and this could ensure that the trust interest binds David. A number of issues have to be considered:

- can a beneficial interest (say, unlike a spousal right of occupation) be protected by actual occupation? Following the classic case of *Williams & Glyn's Bank v Boland*, it is clear that such a trust interest can be protected by the actual occupation of the beneficiary;
- was Norma's trust interest overreached on the sale to David? Overreaching requires two trustees or a trust corporation to receive the purchase money. On the present facts, only John received the purchase money and, therefore, overreaching could not take place and Norma's trust interest remains in Manor House;
- was Norma in actual occupation of Manor House at the date of sale to David? The fact that she was still hospitalised at the time does not entail that she had ceased to occupy. The issue is one of fact and common sense: *Williams & Glyn's Bank v Boland*. Temporary absences, moreover, do not prevent someone being in occupation. The case of *Chhokar v Chhokar* closely resembles the present facts and demonstrates that Norma will still be in actual occupation of Manor House. Reference could also helpfully be made to *Link Lending Ltd v Hussein*;
- does the factual narrative exclude the operation of para.2? It appears that Norma was never asked about her interest in the property by David. It was John who failed to disclose her interest and, indeed, lied to David. Hence, Norma is not tainted by her husband's deception. Her occupation, moreover, would have been obvious on a reasonably careful inspection of Manor House. Her belongings, clothes and personal items would, surely, have alerted David to her occupation. David obviously had no actual knowledge of her occupation.

Accordingly, Norma's interest will bind David.

# Leases

......................................................................................

## 8

## INTRODUCTION

A lease is an estate in land of defined duration. It is capable of being a legal estate under s.1(1)(b) of the **Law of Property Act 1925** provided that it is a "term of years absolute" and is created in the correct manner (i.e. if exceeding three years by deed (ss.52 and 54). If not created by deed, the general rule is that the lease will be equitable in nature. A lease will usually carry with it an estate, but this is not necessarily the case: *Bruton v London & Quadrant Housing Trust* (2000) (see below).

### Terminology

Some of the language associated with leases should be appreciated at the outset:

- the terms lease, term of years, demise and tenancy are interchangeable expressions;
- the landlord is often referred to also as the grantor or lessor;
- the tenant may be described also as the grantee or lessee;
- the landlord's reversion is the estate retained by the landlord on granting the lease;
- an assignment occurs when the tenant or the landlord transfers his entire interest in the property to a new tenant or new landlord as appropriate. For example, T takes a 90-year lease in 2000. In 2010, he sells the remaining 80-year lease to A. As T retains nothing, he has "assigned" his interest in the lease; and
- a subtenancy, sublease or under-lease occurs when the tenant creates a new lease out of his own tenancy (the headlease) which must necessarily be for a period shorter than the remaining period of the headlease. For example, T takes his 90-year lease in 2000 and in 2010 grants S a 20 year sub-tenancy. This is not an assignment because when the 20-year under-lease expires the remaining term of 60 years is not disposed of by T.

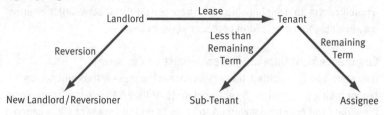

Figure 9: Legal Network

Landlord — Lease → Tenant

Reversion

Less than Remaining Term

Remaining Term

New Landlord/Reversioner     Sub-Tenant     Assignee

## UNUSUAL LEASES

### Perpetually Renewable Leases

A lease in perpetuity is void as it does not constitute a term of years absolute. However, a perpetually renewable lease (i.e. one where the power of renewal is given as often as the lease expires) is saved by s.145 of the **Law of Property Act 1922** and converted into a term of 2000 years. Perpetually renewable leases are created accidentally and inadvertently by giving the tenant, as in *Caerphilly Concrete Products Ltd v Owen* (1972), the right to renew "on the same terms and conditions including this clause" or as in *Northchurch Estate v Daniels* (1947), by granting a renewal "on identical terms and conditions". Only the tenant can terminate the converted 2000 year lease by serving 10 days' notice to quit timed to expire on what would otherwise have been the renewal date.

### Leases for Life or Until Marriage

Under s.149(6) of the **LPA 1925**, a lease at a rent or fine (i.e. a capital premium), for life or lives, or for any term of years determinable with life or lives or on the marriage of the lessee is automatically converted into a 90-year term. Any lease within s.149(6) does not terminate on death or marriage (as the case may be), but instead continues after that time until one party gives at least one month's notice to the other (or heir). The notice must be timed to end on a quarter day (i.e. March 25, June 24, September 29 and December 25).

## THE INGREDIENTS OF A LEASE

### Capable Grantor and Grantee

As made clear in *Rye v Rye* (1962), one cannot lease property to oneself. Where a landlord does not have the legal power to grant tenancies, the agreement cannot confer a leasehold estate: *Camden LBC v Shortlife Community Housing Ltd* (1992). Traditionally, only a licence could then be created, but, following

*Bruton v London & Quadrant Housing Trust* (2000), it is now possible to have a purely contractual relationship which between (and only between) the parties may be categorised as a form of tenancy (see below).

## Commencement Date of the Lease Must be Certain

If no start date is specified, it is assumed that the lease will commence on the tenant taking possession. By virtue of s.149 of the **LPA 1925**, the commencement date can only be delayed up to 21 years (in the meanwhile it is called a reversionary tenancy).

## Duration of the Lease Must be Certain and Capable of being Ascertained

This must be satisfied at the beginning of the lease and explains the policy why perpetual leases and leases for life have been converted by statute into definite periods of years.

## Rent

Although a rent is usual and indicates a lease, it is not necessary: s.205(1)(xxvii) of the **LPA 1925**.

## Exclusive Possession

This is the legal right to exclude all others from the property and must be present for any lease to exist.

## Certainty of Duration
### *Explanation*

With fixed term leases, there is no problem with certainty because the term is expressly defined (e.g. 99 years). As the rule is concerned with maximum duration, a forfeiture clause (which allows the landlord to terminate for breach of tenant's covenant) and a break clause (which allows for early termination at the behest of one or both of the parties) do not offend certainty. In relation to periodic tenancies which run from period to period (e.g. monthly tenancies run from month to month) they too satisfy the certainty requirement and are somewhat artificially viewed as running from, say, month to month until ended by notice to quit.

### *Problematic leases*

If it is impossible to calculate the duration of the term, then the lease is void: *Lace v Chantler* (1944) (a lease for the duration of the war). A lease for the duration of Parliament would, therefore, be invalid. Similarly, a lease to continue until the landlord requires the land for road widening purposes is invalid for uncertainty: *Prudential Assurance Co Ltd v London Residuary Body* (1992). Other uncertain terms have included a lease to continue so long as the company is trading (*Birrel v Carey* (1989)) and until the landlord returns to the UK and makes repayment of a debt (*Canadian Imperial Bank v Bello* (1991)). If a term is void for uncertainty, but the "tenant" has moved in and paid rent then an implied, periodic tenancy may arise instead (see below).

## Exclusive Possession
### *Meaning*

As mentioned, the right to exclusive possession is the right to exclude all others from the premises, including the landlord. Possession relates to legal rights and is not to be confused with "exclusive occupation" which refers merely to physical use. For example, it is possible to have exclusive occupation of a room without being in exclusive possession of it. It is the crucial test employed in distinguishing a lease from a licence agreement. If there is no exclusive possession, there can be no tenancy. The occupier will, instead, have mere permission, i.e. a licence (whether contractual or not) to occupy. If exclusive possession is granted, there will as a general rule be a tenancy. This rule is subject to the limited exceptions considered below.

### *Substance and reality*

The court's approach is to look at the substance and reality of the transaction and to consider the agreement in the factual matrix in which it exists: *Street v Mountford* (1985). Relevant factors will include the relationship between the parties, the nature and extent of the property, the intended and actual use of the property and the real control retained by the landlord. Accordingly, if the grantor remains in general control of the property (as with an inn, hotel or boarding house) a licence is likely to be inferred. Hence, in *Abbeyfield (Harpenden) Society v Woods* (1968) a resident in an old people's home was a licensee because of the services provided and control retained by the management. The subjective intentions of the parties are largely irrelevant. Descriptive labels attached to the agreement are (certainly in the residential market) also far from conclusive.

### *Exclusive possession of what?*

In *Clear Channel UK Ltd v Manchester City Council* (2005), the Court of Appeal demonstrated that, for exclusive possession to exist, the area(s) of land over which the right is said to exist must be capable of precise definition at the date when the right is said to have been created. Here the Council contended successfully that the agreement referred to larger undefined areas of land owned by it and that this indicated only the general location of the advertising displays operated by Clear Channel. Hence, it was not possible to spell out the grant of exclusive possession over specific areas of land occupied by the displays and no tenancy could exist. In short, this case emphasises that there must be certainty of premises for a tenancy to be created.

### Excluding exclusive possession

If the contract attempts to exclude exclusive possession, the court will be watchful for shams, pretences and false terms: *Street v Mountford* (1985). If the attempt is not genuine and realistic, those parts of the agreement will be disregarded: *Antoniades v Villiers* (1990). The court will then give effect to what it considers to be the true bargain. The *Street v Mountford* test extends beyond the residential market and applies in principle also to commercial and agricultural property.

### Beyond the residential

Nevertheless, because of the widely different uses and structures of commercial and agricultural properties, it appears that exclusive possession can in reality be more easily denied: *NCP v Trinity Development* (2001) (a licence of a shoppers' car park). There the Court of Appeal signalled that, in an arm's length agreement between two commercial parties who having been legally advised, the wording of the agreement could be crucial. The parties were to be taken to have appreciated the implications of creating a licence instead of a tenancy. This theme was returned to in *Clear Channel UK Ltd v Manchester City Council* (2005) where Jonathan Parker L.J. agreed that the form of the contract could not be ignored,

> "the fact remains that this was a contract negotiated between two substantial parties of equal bargaining power and with the benefit of full legal advice. Where the contract so negotiated contains not merely a label but a clause which sets out in unequivocal terms the parties' intention as to its legal effect, I would in any event have taken some persuading that its true effect was directly contrary to that expressed intention".

In the commercial field at least, it seems that labels and drafting technique remain of key importance.

### Exceptional situations

In exceptional circumstances, even where exclusive possession exists, a licence rather than a tenancy may be inferred. These instances occur where there is a lack of intention to create legal relations between the parties, for example:

- family arrangements: in *Cobb v Lane* (1952), a brother was allowed to occupy premises and this was held to be a licence and not a tenancy. However, the existence of a family relationship does not automatically prevent a tenancy as can be seen from *Nunn v Dalyrymple* (1990) where a member of the landlord's family was allowed to occupy a cottage in return for regular rent payments and became a tenant. Each situation depends, therefore, upon the intention attributed to the parties and the inferences to be drawn from the circumstances of each case;
- acts of friendship, charity and generosity: in *Booker v Palmer* (1942) a licence was upheld when a homeless woman was allowed to occupy a cottage; see also *Gray v Taylor* (1998) which concerned occupancy of an almshouse; and
- employees: a distinction has to be drawn between an employee who is genuinely required to occupy the premises for the better performance of his duties (e.g. a farm worker in a tied cottage) and an employee who occupies as a fringe benefit or an inducement to encourage the employee to work better. The former potentially falls within the exception (whereby a licence will exist even though exclusive possession is granted) whereas the latter does not: *Norris v Checksfield* (1991).

## Multiple Occupancy Agreements
### Context

Where the premises are occupied by two or more persons, the occupiers will commonly share exclusive possession between themselves and become joint tenants under the lease. For a joint tenancy to exist, however, the so-called four unities (time, possession, title and interest) must be present (see Ch.10).

### Illustrative case

In *AG Securities v Vaughan* (1990), it was possible to fragment the unities so as to prevent a joint tenancy arising. Accordingly, if as here the landlord rents out individual bedrooms in a house to four people previously unconnected with one another and they move in at different times and pay different amounts for the accommodation then no legal alchemy can produce a joint tenancy. None of the four unities were present. If the landlord reserves the right to replace departing occupiers and reallocate rooms, the occupiers are licensees because neither together nor individually can they be said to have exclusive possession. Even if each could be said to have a tenancy of a bedroom, none would enjoy security of tenure because, as they would share essential living rooms, none can be said to occupy a separate dwelling: *Uratemp Ventures v Collins* (2001).

## GRANTING A LEGAL LEASE: FORMALITIES

### Requirements

A legal lease for any period greater than three years can only be created by deed: s.52(1) of the **LPA 1925**. No deed or writing is required at law for a lease which takes effect in possession, is for a term not exceeding three years and is at the best rent reasonably obtainable: s.54(2). The definition by implication also incorporates periodic tenancies. A deed is, however, required for any assignment of a legal lease and this includes one which has been created orally under the three-year exception: *Crago v Julian* (1992).

### Non-compliance

If the parties intend that there be granted a legal lease, but fail to comply with the necessary formalities (i.e. the need for a deed), the lease is equitable. Nevertheless, if either the agreement or the lease is in writing, it will be viewed as a valid contract to create a legal lease. As such, the court can award specific performance of that contract and order the parties to execute a deed. In the intervening period, it is said that "equity looks on that as done which ought to be done" which in *Walsh v Lonsdale* (1882) promoted the conclusion that "an agreement for a lease is as good as a legal lease".

#### *Is a contract just as good?*

An agreement for a lease is not as good as a legal lease for the following reasons:

- a contract is dependent upon the availability of specific performance which is a discretionary remedy and may not be granted if, for example, a tenant is in breach of his obligation: *Coatsworth v Johnson* (1886);
- a legal lease creates an estate enforceable in rem against all third parties, whereas an equitable lease or estate contract is not automatically binding upon a purchaser of the landlord's estate;
- in unregistered land, an equitable lease can be defeated by a bona fide purchaser for value of the legal estate without notice and, moreover, a land contract must be registered as a Civ land charge in order to bind a purchaser for money or money's worth;

- in registered land, an equitable lease and an estate contract are burdens that should be protected by entry on the charges register by virtue of a notice. Protection may also arise under the **Land Registration Act 2002** as, if the equitable tenant is in actual occupation of the property, the tenant may have an overriding interest which binds the purchaser.

## TYPES OF TENANCY

### Periodic Tenancy

Apart from by express agreement, a periodic tenancy may arise by implication in circumstances where a person goes into possession and pays rent. The following observations may be made:

- the precise period of the tenancy is geared according to how the rent is payable. For example, if rent is payable weekly then it is a weekly implied tenancy; if payable monthly it is a monthly tenancy;
- an implied tenancy is a legal term of years absolute and, by virtue of s.54(2) of the **LPA 1925**, does not need to be created by deed; and
- in the absence of contrary agreement, at common law a periodic tenancy can be determined by notice to quit given by either party which is of sufficient duration. With a yearly tenancy the notice is six calendar months; with a quarterly tenancy it is one quarter's notice; with a monthly tenancy it is one month's notice; and with a shorter residential tenancy at least four weeks' notice is required by the **Protection from Eviction Act 1977**.

### Tenancy at Will

This is the lowest estate known to the law because it is determinable at the will of the landlord, it cannot be assigned and terminates upon the death of either party. Such a tenancy can arise expressly or by implication: *Javad v Aqil* (1991). It will usually be found where, with the consent of the landlord, the tenant has either moved into possession or is holding over at the end of a lease pending negotiation of a sale or new lease. A rent may be charged, but such payments are unlikely to convert a genuine tenancy at will into a periodic tenancy: *London Baggage v Railtrack* (2000).

### Tenancy at Sufferance

Where a tenant holds over after the expiry of a lease without the consent or dissent of the landlord, a tenancy at sufferance arises. This is only marginally better than being a trespasser. The landlord can claim possession at any time. The landlord can also claim payment (mesne profits) for the tenant's use and occupation of the land (this payment is not technically to be described as "rent").

## Tenancy by Estoppel

This type of tenancy is based upon the principle that a grantor cannot dispute the validity of the grantee's leasehold title when it would be unconscionable to do so. For a tenancy by estoppel to arise there must be a representation by the landlord that a lease will be created and the tenant must place detrimental reliance upon that representation. This reliance must, however, be reasonable. The fact that the landlord promised only a licence is irrelevant where there is present exclusive possession for a term: *Bruton v London & Quadrant Housing Trust* (2000). As Lord Hoffmann put it, "it is not the estoppel which creates the tenancy, but the tenancy which creates the estoppel". The classic example is where the landlord has no title to grant a lease, but purports to do so. The estoppel will arise on the purported grant and, if the landlord subsequently acquires the relevant title, the lease will be perfected (i.e. the estoppel will be fed).

### Tenancy Without An Estate

The House of Lords in *Bruton v London & Quadrant Housing Trust* (2000) recognised for the first time that it is possible to have a contractual relationship which acts between the parties as a lease, but without conferring on the designated "tenant" any estate in land. In *Bruton*, a licence was granted to the occupier by a landlord who itself had no legal title to grant a tenancy because it also held under a licence. The traditional wisdom was that, as a landlord cannot give a better title than is possessed, Mr Bruton must necessarily be a licensee. His claim to enforce a statutory repairing right available only to tenants, therefore, appeared to be hopeless. Nevertheless, Lord Hoffmann admitted that, although a lease will normally carry with it an estate in land, it need not always do so. He concluded that the relationship of the parties could exist as a tenancy purely within the framework of the contract between them. Hence, he was able to enforce the repair obligations against his landlord. To the outside world, however, Mr Bruton remained a licensee. This contractual tenancy will not, therefore, attract security of tenure and cannot affect third parties: *Kay v London Borough of Lambeth* (2004). It is debatable whether the same decision would have been reached if it had, instead, been the landlord who sought to assert a tenancy against the occupier's wishes (e.g. so as to send bailiffs in to distrain/impound a tenant's goods in lieu of rent payments).

## HOW LEASES END

### Expiry of Time

In a lease for a fixed period, the contractual tenancy will automatically determine when that period expires. Beyond this time, the tenant may have security of tenure (essentially, the right to stay in occupation) afforded by legislation such as the **Rent Act 1977**, the **Housing Act 1988** and Part II of the **Landlord and Tenant Act 1954**.

## Notice to Quit

This is relevant only to periodic tenancies because a lease for a fixed period can only be determined prematurely if the lease so provides. For example, the lease may give either party a right to break a fixed term, say, at the end of the initial five years (this is known as a "break-clause"). As regards residential tenancies, and because of the **Protection from Eviction Act 1977**, the minimum period of notice is four weeks. Otherwise the notice period is that specified in the lease or as required at common law. With the exception of yearly tenancies (where six months' notice is required), the common law requires notice of one full period in order to terminate the contractual tenancy (e.g. a monthly tenancy requires one month's notice). Unless the tenancy is protected by, say, the **Housing Act 1988**, this will suffice to terminate the tenancy: *Mexfield Housing Co-Operative Ltd v Berrisford* (2009). If a joint tenancy exists, a notice to quit served by merely one of them will be valid: *Hammersmith & Fulham LBC v Monk* (1992). A notice to quit given by a tenant will automatically terminate any sub-tenancies which exist: *Pennell v Payne* (1995). The notice given must be clearly worded as, if it would mislead a reasonable landlord or tenant, it will be invalid: *Mannai Investment Co Ltd v Eagle Star Assurance Co Ltd* (1997).

## Merger

This may occur when the freehold estate and leasehold estate become vested in the same person (e.g. if the tenant buys the landlord's reversion). The extinction of the lease is not automatic and is dependent upon merger being intended: See *EDF Energy Networks (EPN) Plc v BoH Ltd* (2009).

## Surrender

It is possible for a tenant to give up the lease to the landlord, that is, to surrender the lease. This can arise expressly (which should be done by deed) or can occur by operation of law (e.g. landlord accepting the return of the tenant's keys: *Chamberlaine v Scally* (1992)). A tenant cannot, however, be forced to offer surrender and a landlord cannot be compelled to accept it. Following surrender, the tenant is released from liability on the covenants (except as to past breaches): *Deanplan v Mahmoud* (1992).

## Disclaimer

This is a predominantly statutory right to repudiate the lease, e.g. a trustee in bankruptcy can disclaim an onerous lease under s.315 of the **Insolvency Act 1986**. Some rights to disclaim put an end to the lease whereas others (including s.315) merely put an end to future liabilities.

# Forfeiture
## *Meaning*

The right to forfeit for breach of tenant's covenant is the most powerful of the landlord's remedies. It allows the landlord to re-enter and put a premature end to the lease. Except as to equitable leases, the right is dependent upon the lease containing a forfeiture clause, i.e. a clause expressly giving the landlord a right to re-enter: *Clarke (Richard) & Co Ltd v Widmall* (1977). It is normal for fixed term leases to contain such a clause.

## *Waiver of breach*

The landlord may, however, waive a breach of covenant either expressly or by conduct and this will prevent forfeiture for that default. Conduct can amount to waiver when the landlord's acts are consistent only with the continued existence of the lease (e.g. if the landlord subsequently sues for or accepts rent: *Central Estates v Woolgar (No. 2)* (1972)). Understandably, the landlord must know of the breach before it can be waived: *Chrisdell v Johnson* (1987). Waiver on one occasion does not operate as a general waiver for continuing breaches in the future: s.148 of the **LPA 1925**.

## Forfeiture Procedures
### *Court order*

Unless the premises are an occupied dwelling, the landlord can physically and peaceably re-enter the land. This is not, however, a popular method of forfeiture and is inappropriate as regards occupied residential premises. Instead, the landlord will institute a forfeiture action in either the county court or, exceptionally, the High Court. The procedure involved is both awkward and complex and the conditions that operate vary according to whether the breach is of a rental covenant or is, instead, of some other covenant.

### *Non-payment of rent*

At common law, it is necessary for the landlord to make a formal demand for the exact sum due on the precise day it falls due. The need for a formal demand is frequently excluded in the lease. If the tenant holds under a long lease (i.e. a lease granted for over 21 years) of a dwelling, the tenant is not obliged to make any payment of rent (usually a ground rent of a low annual sum) unless the landlord serves on him a notice specifying a date for payment between 30 and 60 days hence (ss. 76–77 of the **Commonhold and Leasehold Reform Act 2002**). The landlord will usually serve such a demand automatically twice each year. As regards long residential leases, there are also limits on the landlord's ability to forfeit for arrears of rent or service charge which do not exceed £500.

## Relief

As a general principle, the law leans against forfeiture and will grant relief whenever possible: *Bank of Ireland Home Mortgages v South Lodge* (1997). Relief will be given if the arrears are paid off either before the hearing (automatic) or within a later period specified by the court and it is just and equitable to do so (discretionary). Sub-tenants and mortgagees have a similar right to relief and this is so even if the tenant does not apply for relief. If relief is granted, the landlord may be required to grant a term direct to the sub-tenant or mortgagee for a period not exceeding that which the tenant originally held. An application for relief for breach of rental covenant can be entertained within six months of the landlord's re-taking possession.

## Breach of other covenant

Different considerations apply where the breach is not rent related. Section 146 of the **LPA 1925** provides that the landlord must serve on the tenant a ("last chance") notice which specifies the breach complained of, requires it to be remedied (if capable of being remedied) and demands compensation (unless the landlord waives this). After service of the s.146 notice, the landlord must allow a reasonable period of time (usually three months) for compliance before making a re-entry. As mentioned, it is usually advisable for the landlord to obtain a court order before re-taking possession. As regards long residential leases, the breach must be established before the s.146 notice is served (s.168 of the **Commonhold and Leasehold Reform Act 2002**).

## Incapable of remedy?

Some breaches are incapable of being remedied, e.g. a breach of a covenant against illegal or immoral use which attaches a stigma to the property (*Rugby School Governors v Tannahill* (1935): use of premises as a brothel) and a breach of covenant against assigning, sub-letting or parting with possession (*Scala House and District Property Co v Forbes* (1974)). In such cases, the s.146 notice must specify the breach complained of and should, in order to cater for doubt, require remedy "so far as the same is capable of remedy". Any notice which does not comply with s.146 is void and forfeiture cannot lawfully take place.

*Relief*

The tenant has a right to apply to the court for relief whilst the landlord is proceeding to enforce the forfeiture (i.e. at any time before the landlord has actually re-entered). Unlike with rental breaches, where the court has ordered forfeiture and the landlord has retaken possession, relief ceases to be available (s. 146(2)). If the landlord has, instead, taken the self-help route of peaceable re-entry, a tenant may still apply for relief after a landlord has retaken possession: *Billson v Residential Apartments Ltd* (1992). In deciding whether to grant the tenant (or sub-tenant and tenant's mortgagee as appropriate) relief, the court will take into account all the circumstances of the case.

### Forfeiture for disrepair

If it is a covenant to repair that has been broken, additional formalities are imposed. These extra limitations apply to leases which were granted initially for longer than seven years and which still have at least three years remaining unexpired. The **Leasehold Properties (Repairs) Act 1938** requires the tenant to be told in the s.146 notice of the right to serve a counternotice on the landlord. If a counternotice is served within 28 days of notification, the 1938 Act requires the landlord to obtain the approval of the court before forfeiture can occur. This is particularly advantageous as regards non-residential leases which do not otherwise require the landlord to obtain a court order. The court may allow the landlord to proceed if the value of the freehold has been substantially diminished, the breach needs to be remedied immediately and there are special circumstances that make it just and equitable to allow forfeiture to go ahead.

### Revision Checklist

You should now know and understand:

- the types of lease;
- the ingredients of a lease;
- how to tell a lease from a licence agreement;
- the formalities for creating a legal lease;
- how leases end.

# QUESTION AND ANSWER

Consider the effect of the following limitations in a deed taking effect today:

   i)   to A for one year with an option to renew on the same terms;
   ii)  to B for 21 years or until his death, whichever is the earlier;
   iii) to C for as long as there is a Labour government.

## Advice and the Answer

   i)   The grant is of a term of years absolute within s.1(1) of the **LPA 1925**, i.e. it is a legal lease for one year initially. The reference to the option to renew on the same term raises the question as to whether this creates a perpetually renewable lease. In order for such a lease to exist there has to be a reference to the renewal clause itself, though this has not always been the case as is highlighted in *Northchurch Estates Ltd v Daniels*. There an option to renew "on identical terms and conditions" was held to create a perpetually renewable lease. The current view is that the courts lean against the interpretation of a perpetually renewable lease unless there is a specific reference to the renewal clause itself. Consequently, as there is no specific reference here to the existence of the renewal clause, the better view is that this is a single renewal only. If it is a perpetually renewable lease it would have converted to a term of 2,000 years under s.145 of the **LPA 1922**.

   ii)  For a lease to create a legal term of years absolute within **LPA 1925** s.1(1), it must be created in the correct manner (i.e. by deed, unless it falls within the three-year oral exception created by s.54(2)). For any lease to exist, exclusive possession must be given together with the fact that there is certainty of duration. Here the lease is granted for 21 years, but is determinable on the dropping of a life. If the lease is at a rent or fine it may fall within **LPA 1925** s.149(6), as "a term of years determinable with life or lives" and, as such, would be converted into a 90-year term. If no rent or fine is paid and the lease is gratuitous, the section will not apply and the lease will operate as a term for 21 years determinable on B's death. Such a lease cannot be legal as it contravenes the meaning of "absolute" in s. 205(1) of the **LPA 1925** in that it is determinable on the dropping of a life. Consequently it would be an equitable lease only.

iii) As a pre-requisite of any valid lease there has to be certainty of duration, i.e. the maximum duration of the term must be calculable at the outset. The problem here is that the lease is to terminate on an uncertain event (i.e. Labour ceasing to be the governing party). A series of cases demonstrate the invalidating effect of an uncertainty of term. In *Lace v Chantler* there could be no lease for the duration of the war. In *Canadian Bank v Bello*, there could be no valid lease until the landlord returned from abroad and discharged a debt. Again in *Prudential Assurance v London Residuary* it was held that there could be no lease until the land was needed for road widening purposes. Accordingly, the purported lease fails. Note, however, that if C moves into possession and pays rent then, from the ashes of the failed lease, might arise an implied legal periodic tenancy. This will be geared to how the rent is payable (e.g. if it is payable on a weekly basis, a weekly periodic tenancy will be implied).

# Trusts of Land

........................................................................................................

## 9

## INTRODUCTION

Traditionally, there were two types of trust: the strict settlement under the **Settled Land Act 1925** and the trust for sale under the **Law of Property Act 1925**. Both have now for all practical intents and purposes become obsolete. Since the **Trusts of Land and Appointment of Trustees Act 1996**, these have largely been replaced by the ubiquitous trust of land.

### Successive Interests

Such interests in land were catered for by the strict settlement which is an arrangement which establishes a series of successive beneficial interests in favour of a number of persons. The strict settlement was primarily used to keep land in the family. An example would be where Blackacre is left by a father (A) to his wife (B) for life, remainder to his son (C) in fee simple. A, the person who creates the settlement, is known as the settlor; B is the tenant for life; and C is known as the remainderman. C will become absolutely entitled to the property when B dies. The **Trusts of Land and Appointment of Trustees Act 1996,** however, prevents the creation of any new strict settlements. The settlement has been an undesirable and outmoded method of landholding. As a result, it is rarely taught in any depth these days and need not detain us further within this chapter.

### Concurrent Interests

Traditionally these operated behind a trust for sale under which the duty of the trustees was to sell the land subject to the trust. This too has effectively been abolished by the 1996 Act and existing trusts for sale are converted into the simpler and newly styled trusts of land (under which the trustees have merely a power to sell). In addition, the doctrine of conversion (whereby a beneficiary's interest under the old style trust for sale was automatically deemed not to be in the land, but rather in the proceeds of an eventual sale of the land) is abandoned by s.3. It is with the trust of land that this chapter is concerned.

# THE TRUST OF LAND

## Background

With the **Trusts of Land and Appointment of Trustees Act 1996** a new and unified approach to land trusts dawned. The Act defines a trust of land as "any trust of property which consists of or includes land". The Act applies to all forms of trust whether express, resulting or constructive. The beneficiaries under the trust of land hold an interest in the land (albeit equitable) and not in money proceeds: s.3. One consequence of this is that beneficial ownership has become a property right and is now within the definition of land in s.205(1)(ix) of the **LPA 1925**.

## Trustees' Functions

The powers and functions of the trustees focus upon the management of, and dealings with, the trust property. Under s.6(1) of the 1996 Act, legal title will be vested in the trustees and it is they who will have all the powers of an absolute owner for the purpose of exercising their functions as trustees. The powers of the trustees may, however, be excluded, modified or made subject to the consent of the beneficiaries, but only if this is provided for by the trust instrument or order of the court (s.8).

## Powers and Duties

- trustees' powers include the ability to sell, to mortgage or to lease the property and to purchase land (s.6); to divide physically (i.e. partition) the trust property between the beneficiaries so that each beneficiary can own a separate part (s.7); to exclude a beneficiary from occupation of the property (s.13); to apply to court if there is a dispute between the trustee and the beneficiaries (s.14) and to delegate powers to a beneficiary (s.9);
- the trustees owe a duty to exercise reasonable skill and care imposed by the **Trustee Act 2000**;
- the trustees' powers are fiduciary in nature which essentially means that they must be exercised honestly, impartially and without personal advantage. This means that, in exercising their powers, the trustees shall have regard to the rights and interests of the beneficiaries (s.6(5)); and
- when exercising any function relating to land subject to the trust, s.11(1) imposes on the trustees a duty, so far as is practicable, to consult with the beneficiaries of full age and, in so far as is consistent with the purposes of the trust, to give effect to their wishes. When a new trust of land is created, the creators of the trust can "opt out" of the consultation obligation. Similarly, pre-existing trusts can be "opted in".

## Beneficiary's Rights

The beneficiary under a trust of land has a variety of rights:

- the qualified s.12 right to occupy the land (discussed below);
- where all the beneficiaries are of full age and act unanimously, the s.19 right to appoint and remove trustees;
- the s.11 right to be consulted about the exercise of the trustees' functions (in the absence of consultation, it is possible that a beneficiary could obtain an injunction restraining the trustees' actions): *Waller v Waller* (1967);
- the s.14 right to apply for a court order in times of dispute between the trustees and a beneficiary; and
- the right to an appropriate share in the capital money following the sale of the trust land.

## Occupation Rights

The 1996 Act attempts to state comprehensively the entitlement of beneficiaries to occupy the co-owned property. It confers a right of occupation and then specifies the circumstances in which it can be cancelled or modified. Section 12 allows a beneficiary to occupy the land at any time provided the land is available for occupation and occupation is not inconsistent with the trust of land. There is no s.12 right if the property is unavailable or unsuitable for occupation. In *Chan v Leung* (2003), a couple separated and the issue was whether Ms Leung had a right to continue in short term occupation of the co-owned property. It was argued that the house was so large that it was unsuitable for her sole occupation. This argument was rejected by the Court of Appeal which was of the opinion that, as she had lived there previously, it would now be difficult to show unsuitability. A co-owner with legal title already has the right to occupy by virtue of having the legal estate.

### Restrictions

The right to occupy might be restricted under s.13 where there are two or more beneficiaries. The trustees might then exclude the entitlement of one or more beneficiaries (but not them all: *Rodway v Landy* (2001)) to occupy. A co-owner already in occupation can be excluded only with his consent or by an order of the court (s.13(7)). The trustees are required to act reasonably which means that they must, by virtue of s.13(4) consider the intentions of the person(s) who created the trust, the purpose for which the land is held and the circumstances and wishes of each beneficiary who is otherwise entitled to occupy the property.

### *Conditions*

The trustees can attach conditions to a beneficiary's right to occupy: s.13(3). These conditions must be reasonable and can include a requirement that the occupying beneficiary pays all outgoings and expenses in relation to the land (see *Rodway v Landy* (2001)). If a beneficiary is excluded from the land, the occupiers might be required by the trustee to pay a rent (by way of compensation for loss of the right) to an excluded co-owner: s.13(6).

**Figure 10: Trusts of Land: Key Rights**

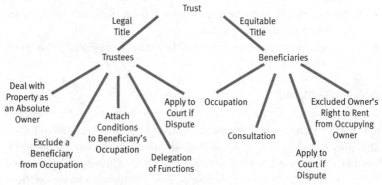

## SALE OF TRUST LAND

### Trustees' Power to Sell

Trustees have wide powers of sale should they choose to exercise them. If the trustees cannot agree as to whether the land should be sold they, or any interested party, may apply to the court for it to make such order as it thinks fit: s.14 of the 1996 Act. If the trustees choose to exercise the power to sell, they have all the powers of an absolute owner. On a sale the proceeds are held for the beneficiaries whose interests in the land are likely to be overreached by the purchaser. Before exercising any power of sale, the trustees must obtain any consents required by the trust instrument and have consulted with the beneficiaries. After consultation the trustees should normally give effect to the wishes of the beneficiaries.

### Sale by Court Order
#### *Disputes*

On the breakdown of a relationship, for example, one co-owner might want to sell the land and distribute the proceeds of sale between them. Another co-owner may not wish to sell and may seek to continue in residence. The 1996 Act caters generally for the court to resolve disputes as between co-owners themselves and as between co-owners and trustees (e.g. as to the exercise of the trustees' functions).

## Considerations

As regards such disputes, s.15(1) provides a list of factors for the court to take into account. These are:

- the intentions of the creators of the trust;
- the purposes for which the property subject to the trust is held;
- the welfare of any minor who occupies or might reasonably be expected to occupy the land; and
- the interests of any secured creditor of any beneficiary.

## Example

If, say, a couple who own a house together separate, the purpose of the trust (to provide a home for them both) has clearly ceased and the court may well be persuaded to order sale (as in *Jones v Challenger* (1961)). If, however, the couple have a young child then sale might be postponed possibly until the child reaches school leaving age (as in *Re Evers' Trust* (1980)). To minimise hardship to the party who might be required to move out, the court could order a rent to be paid to the excluded co-owner: s.13(6).

## Illustrative cases

- In *Re Buchanan-Wollaston's Conveyance* (1939), there were four neighbouring property owners who combined to buy a piece of land that they desired to keep as an open space. The land was conveyed to them as joint tenants. The parties entered into a covenant in which they agreed to preserve the open space. One party wanted to sell up and applied to have the communal property sold. The court refused a sale as it would not allow a man in breach of his obligation to prevail.
- In *Harris v Harris* (1996) the conclusive factor in determining that the land should not be sold was the fact that the express trust deed stipulated that the property was to provide a home for father and son as long as either of them wished to stay there. Although their relationship had broken down, the purpose of the trust still survived.

## Sale on Insolvency
*Context*

If the dispute as to sale is between the co-owners and a trustee in bankruptcy of one of them, very different considerations apply: s.15(4). The general rule is that the interests of the creditors should prevail and that sale should be ordered by the court: *Re Citro* (1991). This leaning in favour of the creditors is explicitly recognised in s.335A(2) of the **Insolvency Act 1986**. The bankruptcy court will deal with the matter and is obliged to make an order which is "just and reasonable" having regard to the interests of the creditor and the conduct and financial resources of the bankrupt's spouse (or former spouse), the needs of any children and all other circumstances. The needs of the bankrupt are, however, excluded from this consideration.

*Timing*

If an application for sale is made more than one year after bankruptcy, the court must award sale unless the circumstances are exceptional. Sale might be refused, for example, where there is a resident child who is disabled or suffers from a terminal or serious long-term illness: *Re Bailey* (1977). In *Re Bremner* (1999), the bankrupt was dying of cancer and the court postponed sale until three months after his death. In *Re Citro*, however, the loss of a home and the need to change schools were not "exceptional" circumstances.

## PURCHASER PROTECTION

### Overreaching and the Two Trustee Rule
The overreaching provisions in s.2 of the **LPA 1925** apply so that if a purchaser pays capital money to at least two trustees or a trust corporation his interest prevails over any equitable interests arising under the trust. This applies both to unregistered and registered land: *City of London Building Society v Flegg* (1986). On termination of a trust, the trustees might be required to execute a deed of discharge. A purchaser will not need to check that trustees have obtained any consents required, consulted with beneficiaries or have acted in the best interests of any beneficiaries.

### Single Trustee: Unregistered Land
The equitable interest created under a trust of land is not registrable by way of a land charge and is subject to the overreaching machinery. Of course, in the case of a single legal owner overreaching does not apply. In that situation whether the co-owners interest will bind turns, instead, upon the equitable

doctrine of notice. There has been some dispute as to when a purchaser of unregistered land has constructive notice of the rights of an occupying spouse. In *Caunce v Caunce* (1969), the presence of a wife in the matrimonial home was deemed not to constitute notice to the purchaser. The purchaser was not expected to act as a "snooper" and "busybody". This rule was criticised in *Williams & Glyn's Bank Ltd v Boland* (1981) and *Kingsnorth Finance v Tizard* (1986) and the modern view is that, as a wife's presence is separate from that of her husband, her occupation in the property is deemed to give constructive notice to the purchaser. This is so only when her presence should have been detected on a reasonably careful inspection of the property.

### Sole survivor

Where there is a sole survivor in both law (legal title) and equity (beneficial title) a purchaser of unregistered land is protected and will obtain good title if he pays the proceeds of sale to the single trustee. This is because of the **Law of Property (Joint Tenants) Act 1964**, as amended, which provides that a purchaser from a surviving joint tenant will get a good title, free from any trust interest created, if the surviving joint tenant conveys as beneficial owner. A purchaser will not, in those circumstances, need to appoint a second trustee so as to effect overreaching. The protection of the 1964 Act does not extend to registered land.

## Single Trustee: Registered Land

In the absence of overreaching, the interest of a co-owner in occupation of the family home can bind a purchaser. Section 26 of the **Land Registration Act 2002**, however, provides a general shield for purchasers against adverse claims that are not entered on the register and are not overriding interests. A trust interest cannot be noted on the register by entry of a notice, but a beneficiary or the Land Registrar can enter a restriction. Hence, the existence of another's beneficial interest should be revealed by this type of entry. If no restriction is entered, the purchaser will normally get a good title. The exception to this is when the co-owner is in actual occupation and benefits from an overriding interest binding on the purchaser.

---

### KEY CASE

In *Williams & Glyn's Bank Ltd v Boland* (1981), a husband held the matrimonial home on trust for sale for himself and his wife. He mortgaged the house to the Bank and defaulted on the repayments. The Bank sought to take possession, prior to selling the property. Mrs Boland argued that she had a beneficial interest which, because of her actual occupation, was binding on the Bank. The House of Lords held that her interest did, indeed, bind the Bank. This is because her rights, as a person in actual occupation, constituted an overriding interest and did not need to be otherwise protected in order to bind a purchaser (see further Ch.7).

## Revision Checklist

You should now know and understand:

- **the meaning of a trust of land;**

- **the functions of a trustee;**

- **the rights of a beneficiary;**

- **the circumstances in which trust land may be sold;**

- **the protections afforded to a purchaser of trust land.**

# QUESTION AND ANSWER

## Question

John and Don are the joint legal and equitable owners of Paradise House. They purchased the property in 2004 as a joint home for themselves and Don's son, Carter. Last year, John moved out of Paradise House in order to live with his girlfriend, Zena. John now wishes for the property to be sold, but Don refuses to consent to sale.

Fiona and Keith are the co-owners of the Cottage. They have a child, Vinnie, who is terminally ill. Fiona has recently become bankrupt, owing creditors £150,000. Fiona's trustee in bankruptcy now seeks to enforce sale of the Cottage. Fiona and Keith intend to resist proceedings and wish to remain in occupation of the family home. They claim that moving house would risk their son's life.

Advise John and Fiona and Keith.

## Advice and the Answer

In both scenarios there is necessarily a trust of land because co-ownership can only occur behind such a vehicle. Legal title is vested in the trustees

(Don & John; Keith & Fiona) and they hold the land on trust for themselves beneficially (i.e. these characters are both trustees and beneficiaries).

In relation to Don and John, both have a right to occupy Paradise House as they have joint legal title and also by virtue of s.12 of the **TOLATA**. There is, of course, no obligation to reside in the premises. There is also here no question of a co-owner being excluded from occupation. The issue instead focuses upon the continuing occupation of Don and the possible sale of the premises against Don's wishes. As regards the former, it is possible that, under s.13, the trustees may agree or the court order that restrictions be placed upon John's continuing occupation (e.g. that Don pays the outgoings of the property and possibly a rent to compensate John for the loss of use of Paradise House). The rent will become particularly relevant if sale is not ordered. In relation to sale, John will have to apply to the court under s.14 for an order of sale. The court enjoys the discretion whether or not to order sale, but that discretion is influenced by a series of factors listed in s.15. These include such factors as the purposes for which the property was bought, the original intentions of the parties and the welfare of any minor occupying the property (i.e. Carter). Pointers towards sale would be that the home sharing relationship has ended and that it was the intention that the house provides a home for both purchasers (*Jones v Challenger*). The major obstacle to sale is the presence of Carter. It may be that the court will place emphasis on safeguarding the child's interests and refuse to order sale until Carter has reached school leaving age (*Re Ever's Trust*). It is perhaps significant that the child is not also John's and that Paradise House was not intended to provide a traditional family home.

Keith and Fiona are in a very different position. They do not wish to sell the property and both wish to continue in occupation. A new dynamic, however, is introduced by the participation of the trustee in bankruptcy. This involvement brings with it a different set of considerations as s.15(4) makes clear that the provisions of s.335A of the **Insolvency Act** apply instead. This entails that the court will reach its decision on the basis of what is "just and reasonable" while balancing the interests of the creditors and the interests of the bankrupt's family. In this scenario, the interests of the creditors will normally prevail (*Re Citro*). The chances of remaining in the family home are greater until the first anniversary of the bankruptcy. After that time the court must order sale unless the circumstances are "exceptional". Fiona would, therefore, point to her son's terminal illness and argue that, as in *Re Bailey*, the health hazards posed by his moving house constituted a sufficiently exceptional situation. If this argument prevails, it is likely that, as in *Re Bremner*, the court would postpone sale until some months after Vinnie's death.

# Co-ownership

..........................................................................................................

## 10

## INTRODUCTION

This Chapter deals with the concurrent co-ownership of land, that is, where two or more persons are entitled to simultaneous enjoyment of land. For example, the grant of Blackacre "to X and Y in fee simple" or "to X and Y in equal shares" creates co-ownership. As shown in the Ch.9, this is in contrast to where land is granted consecutively as "to X for life, then to Y in fee simple" which traditionally created a strict settlement. The law relating to co-ownership can be found in the common law rules, the structures of the 1925 property legislation and the provisions of the **Trusts of Land and Appointment of Trustees Act 1996**. There are two types of co-ownership in land that have modern significance: the joint tenancy and the tenancy in common. It is to be appreciated that the use of the word "tenancy" here refers to ownership of a freehold or leasehold estate and is not an allusion to the landlord and tenant context.

..........................................................................................................

## THE JOINT TENANCY

### DEFINITION CHECKPOINT

In the eyes of the law, joint tenants do not have shares in the land or, indeed, any individual existence. They are regarded together as making up a single legal entity, i.e. a sole owner: *Burton v Camden LBC* (2000). They are together wholly entitled, but individually they own nothing. Of course, they do have rights which are exercisable against each other (e.g. a monetary claim on any eventual sale). The joint tenancy is favoured by the common law. The outstanding feature of the joint tenancy is the right of survivorship (ius accrescendi).

### Survivorship

On the death of one joint tenant, his interest in land passes to the survivors automatically by right of survivorship. This process continues until eventually only one owner survives. At that point, co-ownership ceases and the sole survivor becomes absolutely entitled to the land. There is no conveyance, no probate and no death duties to be paid. The right of survivorship, moreover, is not ousted by a joint tenant's will or by the intestacy rules. The right of survivorship might be advisable in relation to the family home, but is clearly unsuited to an investment venture between partners or friends.

## The Four Unities
A joint tenancy cannot exist unless the four unities exist: *AG Securities v Vaughan* (1990).

### Unity of possession

Each co-owner must be entitled to possession of any part of the land and entitled to possession of the whole land with the others. This does not mean that the co-owners must all actually occupy the property. If one occupier moves out, a joint tenancy will continue unaffected. It is to do with legal entitlement (which Parliament can modify, e.g. under domestic violence legislation or under the **Trusts of Land and Appointment of Trustees Act 1996**) and not mere de facto use.

### Unity of interest

The interest of each joint tenant must be identical in extent, nature and duration. One cannot have a larger interest than another as together they are entitled to the whole. No joint tenancy is, therefore, possible between a freeholder and a leaseholder. Similarly no single joint tenant can sell or lease the land because he does not have the whole legal estate. An attempt to do so might amount to a severing event (see below). All the joint tenants must assent and join in the transaction. Similarly, the surrender of a lease must be made by all joint tenants as must the exercise of a break clause in a lease. Paradoxically, a notice to quit under a periodic lease given by one of several joint tenants will be valid: *Hammersmith and Fulham LBC v Monk* (1992). As each new period amounts to a renewal of the lease, the unwillingness of one joint tenant is fatal to the continuance of the lease.

### Unity of title

All joint tenants must claim title under the same act or document, for example, by the same act of adverse possession or by the same conveyance.

### Unity of time

The interests of the joint tenants must all vest (i.e. be acquired) at the same time.

## Consequences of a Joint Tenancy

A joint tenancy has the following features:

- each co-owner has a "prospective" share in the property. If there are four co-owners, each has a potential one-quarter share of the proceeds of sale. They are entitled to any rents and profits pending sale in the same proportions;
- the joint tenancy will continue until only one survivor is entitled to the land by way of survivorship; and
- any joint tenant can convert his joint tenancy into a tenancy in common by way of severance (see below).

## THE TENANCY IN COMMON

### Differences from a Joint Tenancy

This form of co-ownership is favoured by equity and entails that each co-owner has a separate share in the property. A tenancy in common differs from a joint tenancy in the following ways:

- tenants in common hold in individual shares, i.e. they have distinct, notional shares in the land that has not yet been divided between the co-owners. Although each tenant in common has a separate interest, it is not possible to say who owns what piece of the land;
- there is no right of survivorship. The size of share of a tenant in common is fixed and unaffected by the death of any other tenant in common. The tenant in common can leave his share by will and, if not, it will pass on intestacy to his next of kin;
- of the four unities only unity of possession is essential. Without this there can be no co-ownership at all. There would, instead, be individual ownership of distinct parts;
- the size of the shares of each tenant in common need not be equal. For example, one tenant in common may have a 60 per cent share whereas the other may have a 40 per cent stake.

## THE LEGAL FRAMEWORK

All forms of co-ownership must exist behind a trust of land: ss.4–5 of the **Trusts of Land and Appointment of Trustees Act 1996**. This means that there is a fragmentation of legal and equitable ownership.

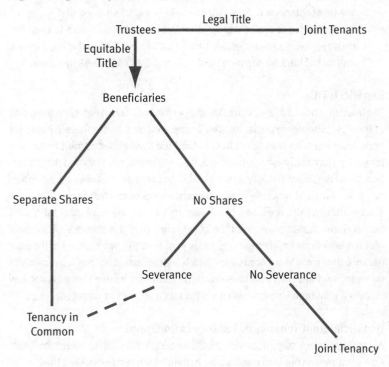

## Legal Title

The legal estate (i.e. paper title) must be held by one or more trustees. If there is more than one trustee, the legal title must always be held as joint tenants. There are no exceptions to this rule. There can be no tenancy in common of the legal estate: s.1(6) of the **Law of Property Act 1925**. It is impossible, therefore, to convert a joint tenancy at law into a tenancy in common at law.

### Numbers

There can only be a maximum of four trustees who hold the legal estate in land. The trustees will be named in the conveyance and, if more than four are named, the legal estate is vested in the first four named in the conveyance who are of full age and capacity and who are willing to act: s.34(2) of the **Trustee Act 1925**. The following examples serve to illustrate:

- a conveyance to A and B who are of full age and capacity. A and B hold the legal estate as trustees on a statutory trust of land as joint tenants at law for the benefits of themselves as co-owners in equity;

- a similar conveyance to A, B, C, D and E. Here the first four named hold the legal estate as trustees for the benefit of all five in equity;
- a conveyance to X and Y to hold for the benefit of A, B and C. Here the trustees have been expressly named and X and Y hold the legal estate on trust of land for the benefit of A, B and C as co-owners in equity.

## Beneficial Title

The trustee(s) hold the legal estate for the persons entitled in equity on the terms of the trust whether express, implied or imposed by statute. The equitable (or beneficial) interests may take effect behind the trust either as joint tenants or tenants in common. It is here, therefore, that true entitlement lies and the distinction between a joint tenancy and a tenancy in common assumes major importance. Working out which type of co-ownership has been created will turn upon such matters as the presence of the four unities (all are necessary for a joint tenancy), the stated purpose of the conveyance (e.g. it may expressly declare that the beneficial entitlement is to be as joint tenants), words used in the conveyance (there might be words used which are consistent only with a tenancy in common) and any presumptions which the court may invoke (the common law favours a joint tenancy whereas equity favours a tenancy in common).

## Beneficial Joint Tenancy or Tenancy in Common?

As indicated a four-stage approach should be adopted in order to determine which type of co-ownership is to regulate the beneficial interests under the trust.

### Are the four unities present?

If so, then it can be a joint tenancy. If not, it most certainly cannot be a joint tenancy. This means that the four unities are a necessary, but not decisive, condition for the existence of a joint tenancy.

### Is there an express declaration in the conveyance?

If the parties declare themselves to be joint tenants or to be tenants in common, this will usually be decisive: *Roy v Roy* (1996). For example "to A, B, C and D as joint tenants at law and in equity" will normally be conclusive of a joint tenancy. If the conveyance declares the existence of a tenancy in common, this will always be decisive.

### Are any words of severance used in the grant?

Words of severance are terms and expressions that clearly indicate a tenancy in common. Examples would include, share, equally, amongst and divided between.

In *Martin v Martin* (1987) a tenancy in common emerged as the words "in equal shares" were used. These words indicate that the co-owners have separate interests in the land.

### Are there any evidential presumptions which can help the court?

The common law presumes that a joint tenancy has been created and the general rule is that this presumption will prevail. The rule gives way, however, in limited circumstances when equity will intervene. This limited intervention will arise where:

- the purchase money is provided in unequal shares, a tenancy in common in proportion to the share of the money advanced is presumed: *Bull v Bull* (1955). In *Malayan Credit Ltd v Jack Chia- MPH Ltd* (1986), rent payable in unequal shares was equivalent to providing the purchase money in unequal shares and, therefore, a tenancy in common was presumed; or
- the land is acquired by business partners as part of partnership assets a tenancy in common is presumed: *Lake v Craddock* (1732). No formal partnership is required and the rule applies to any joint undertaking with a view to profit. The right of survivorship has no place in commerce.

## Severance of the Joint Tenancy

It is to be remembered that the legal estate must always be held on a joint tenancy and cannot be severed, i.e. converted into a tenancy in common. Severance is only possible in respect of the beneficial interests of the co-owners. A joint tenancy behind a trust can be converted into a tenancy in common in a number of ways.

### Acting upon one's share

The clearest method of severance is to alienate (sell or otherwise dispose of) one's own interest to a stranger or, indeed, another joint tenant. This must occur inter vivos (i.e. be a lifetime dealing) and cannot, therefore, be effected by a will. The act must be final and binding which means that there must generally be a valid contract/written transfer dealing with the land. A mere statement of intention is insufficient. It is to be appreciated that:

- where a joint tenant sells his potential share, the purchaser becomes a tenant in common as to that share and other joint tenants (provided there are more than one) remain joint tenants as to the rest of the estate;
- the alienation may be involuntary, for example, where the interest in the joint tenancy passes to a trustee in bankruptcy on insolvency: *Re Dennis* (1996);

- the alienation may be partial, e.g. mortgaging one's share or creating a lease or life interest will sever the joint tenancy; and
- the alienation may arise following the commencement of litigation and may amount to an act upon one's share provided that the court action directly concerns the joint tenancy itself. Merely commencing divorce proceedings, for example, would not sever a joint tenancy between estranged husband and wife.

### Mutual agreement of the joint tenants

The joint tenants can all act together and effectively agree to sever their joint tenancy: *Williams v Hensman* (1861). This is more informal than acting on one's share and does not need a valid contract or writing. It must, however, be such that it shows a common intention to sever. The parties must have reached a definite understanding and a fixed mutual attitude to sever: *Slater v Slater* (1987). For example, if the joint tenants agree that, on death, their shares will pass to their next of kin this will be a severing event: *McDonald v Morley* (1940). Similarly, if the joint tenants agree that, on sale, the proceeds should be divided (whether equally or unequally) a tenancy in common will immediately arise: *Burgess v Rawnsley* (1975).

### Mutual conduct of all existing joint tenants

This covers any course of dealing which intimates that the interests of all joint tenants were mutually regarded as having been severed. The conduct must fall short of an express or implied agreement, but must show an unambiguous, common intention to sever: *Greenfield v Greenfield* (1979). For example, where the co-owners execute mutual wills it is not the wills themselves which sever (severance cannot be effected by will); but rather the intention which underlies them shows the decision to sever: *Re Wilford's Estate* (1879). It is not entirely clear whether inconclusive negotiations in relation to disposing of the co-owners' respective shares will operate to sever the joint tenancy. The better view is that such negotiations will not have this effect: *Harris v Goddard* (1983).

### Homicide

A person cannot benefit from his crime so that if one joint tenant unlawfully kills another he cannot take any benefit by way of survivorship: *Cleaver v Mutual Reserve Fund* (1892). Section 2(2) of the Forfeiture Act 1982, however, gives the court a limited discretion to override this rule (but not with murder) where it is just to do so (as in *Dunbar v Plant* (1998): suicide pact). It appears that the consequences of the forfeiture rule will vary according to how many other joint tenants remain alive. Consider the following examples:

- A and B hold as joint tenants at law and in equity. A murders B. A then holds the legal estate for himself and the estate of B as tenants in common in equity;
- A, B and C hold as joint tenants at law and in equity. A murders B. A and C hold the legal estate as joint tenants on trust for B's estate and themselves as tenants in common. If A and C were allowed to remain as joint tenants, it would mean that A achieved some potential benefit from his crime (i.e. the tontine effect: there would be one less joint tenant to take under the right of survivorship); and
- A, B, C and D hold as joint tenants at law and in equity and A murders B. A, C and D hold the legal estate as joint tenants on trust for A and B's estate as tenants in common and for C and D as joint tenants. Neither C nor D has committed any wrongdoing and neither profit from their own actions. It would be unfair on C and D, as well as being illogical, if their joint tenancy was severed by the criminal activity of A.

### Notice in writing under section 36(2) of the LPA 1925

If a joint tenant desires to sever the joint tenancy unilaterally he can achieve this by giving all the other joint tenants clear notice in writing of this desire. The notice must show an immediate intention to sever and not merely be a statement of future aspiration: *Harris v Goddard* (1983). A notice which has been posted, but not received remains effective for these purposes: *Re 88 Berkeley Road* (1971). In *Kinch v Bullard* (1998), a wife posted a letter notifying severance to her husband in respect of the matrimonial home. The husband was dying in hospital at the time and did not receive the notice. The wife thought she would now prosper better with the right of survivorship and destroyed the notice. The court held that there was severance despite the fact that the husband never actually received the notice. In *Re Drapers Conveyance* (1969), the issue of a summons by a wife claiming a sale of the matrimonial home amounted to notice for this purpose. In *Harris v Goddard* (1983), however, no severance occurred where a divorce petition had been served on a husband which merely stated that an order might be made at a future time in respect of the matrimonial home.

### Termination of Co-ownership

Co-ownership can end in a variety of ways:

*Partition*

This is a mechanism whereby the land is physically divided between the co-owners. The joint tenants must be of full age and partition must normally be effected by deed. On partition each co-owner becomes absolutely entitled to a separate plot of land. Under s.7 of the **Trusts of Land and Appointment of Trustees Act 1996,** the trustees of land have powers of partition.

*Overreaching*

Where the trustees transfer title to a purchaser, and the purchase money is paid to at least two trustees or a trust corporation, the beneficiaries' interests are overreached and the co-ownership terminates.

*Union in sole ownership (merger)*

This will occur where all the legal and beneficial interests are finally vested in one person. For example, when only one joint tenant remains alive, when there is release by one joint tenant of his interest to the other and where tenants in common leave their interest by will or intestacy to a remaining co-owner.

## BENEFICIARIES AND MORTGAGE LENDERS

Much litigation has concerned an occupier with a beneficial interest attempting to enforce that interest against a mortgagee. A major distinction has emerged from these cases and this turns upon whether or not the mortgage is to finance the acquisition of the property.

### Acquisition Mortgages

When the mortgage is entered in order to finance the initial purchase of the family home (i.e. an acquisition mortgage), the lender is in the strongest position:

- the occupier will not usually be in occupation at the key time when the mortgage is created and so the chances of the occupier having a binding interest are reduced: *Abbey National Building Society v Cann* (1991);

- the beneficial co-owner will or should know that the purchase is mortgage assisted and is, therefore, deemed to have consented to his rights being relegated behind those of a mortgagee: *Paddington Building Society v Mendelsohn* (1985); and

- once consent to the original mortgage is given or implied, that consent will extend to a later re-mortgage, but only up to the same amount: *Equity & Law Home Loans Ltd v Prestridge* (1992).

## Non-Acquisition Mortgages

When the mortgage is not contemporaneous with the purchase (i.e. it is what is called a second mortgage or non-acquisition mortgage), the lender is more vulnerable:

- the beneficial co-owner will now, in all likelihood, be in occupation;
- subject to overreaching, the lender in the capacity of purchaser will, therefore, have constructive notice of the trust interest (unregistered land) or take subject to it as an interest that overrides registration (registered land); and
- the lender will try to protect itself against such claims by obtaining from all occupiers an express disclaimer of their rights. This disclaimer of rights will be overturned only if it was induced by the misrepresentation and/ or undue influence of the borrower: *Barclays Bank v O'Brien* (1994).

## Wrongdoing and the Mortgagee

A mortgage lender will be affected by the wrongdoing of another (e.g. duress, misrepresentation or undue influence) when the loan appears not to be to the benefit of the complainant (e.g. where a wife puts at risk the matrimonial home in order to guarantee her husband's business debts). In such cases, the lender is put on inquiry that some wrongdoing may have occurred. The wife here is acting as a surety for her husband, i.e. placing at risk her share in the family home for no direct benefit for herself. Obviously, if the expressed purpose of the loan is for the joint benefit of the husband and wife (e.g. to buy a car or a holiday home), there is nothing that can put the lender on inquiry. Nevertheless, once put on inquiry, and before the transaction goes ahead, the lender is expected to take reasonable steps to protect itself and to ensure that the vulnerable party understands the risks of the proposed loan. Lord Nicholls in *Royal Bank of Scotland Plc v Etridge (No.2)* (2001) set out the steps that the lender and the legal adviser must take.

### *The lender*

The lender must communicate with the surety (preferably at a face to face meeting) and inform the surety of the need to obtain independent legal advice and request her to nominate a solicitor. The lender should not proceed until it has received an appropriate response from the surety. The lender must supply to the adviser sufficient information about the proposed transaction and the financial standing of the principal borrower. If the lender suspects that there has been wrongdoing, it should inform the legal adviser accordingly. If the lender knows of any vulnerability of the surety (e.g. that she does not speak English), this must also be communicated.

### The adviser

The adviser must explain the risk of the transaction to the surety and this must be done in non-technical language at a face to face meeting. The advice should address what are termed the core minimum issues which include an explanation of the legal effect of the documents and their contents, an inquiry into the surety's financial means, a discussion as to the principal borrower's financial means, an offer to negotiate directly with the lender as to revised terms and a reminder that the surety does not have to proceed with the transaction. The adviser should not assure the lender that the transaction has been explained without the express authority of the surety.

### The lender

The lender should not proceed with the loan unless and until the adviser certifies that the transaction has been explained to the surety. If it does proceed without this assurance, it is not shielded from any subsequent claims as to wrongdoing made by the surety. If it waits until certification, the lender will usually be protected and any claims made by the surety will be directed at her adviser on the basis of negligence and/or breach of contract.

### Revision Checklist

You should now know and understand:

- **the trust mechanism which underpins co-ownership of land;**
- **the differences between a joint tenancy and a tenancy in common;**
- **how to identify a joint tenancy from a tenancy in common;**
- **the methods by which an equitable joint tenancy may be severed;**
- **the ability of a mortgage lender to enforce its rights against a co-owner.**

# QUESTION AND ANSWER

## Question

Gerald, Harry, James, Kitty and Leslie bought a vacant plot of unregistered land known as "Keele Lodge" from Natalie in 2000 hoping its value would increase. The conveyance, which the parties prepared without professional advice purported to convey the land "to Gerald, Harry, James, Kitty and Leslie as joint tenants in law and equity". The purchasers provided the purchase money equally.

In 2001, Kitty died and the following year Harry purchased James' interest. In 2005, Harry died, appointing James as his executor. Recently Leslie orally agreed to purchase Gerald's interest in the property for £75,000.

Explain the devolution of the legal estate and of the equitable interests in "Keele Lodge".

## Advice and the Answer

The conveyance of the property to Gerald, Harry, James, Kitty and Leslie creates a form of co-ownership, which is where land is conveyed to two or more persons simultaneously. Such co-ownership creates a trust of land under the provisions of the **Trusts of Land and Appointment of Trustees Act 1996**. The trustees of the co-owned property will hold the legal estate on a joint tenancy for the benefit of the equitable owners.

The legal estate is always held as an unseverable joint tenancy under the trust of land created by ss.34 and 36 of the **LPA 1925**. If no trustees are specifically appointed, the first four individuals named in the conveyance who are of full age and capacity will hold the legal estate as trustees. There can be no more than four trustees in this situation: s.34(2) of the **LPA 1925**. Consequently, Gerald, Harry, James and Kitty will hold the legal estate for the benefit of Gerald, Harry, James, Kitty and Leslie in equity. The use of a trust simplifies conveyancing in that it enables a purchaser to deal only with the trustees and to effectively take free of the interests of the beneficiaries.

In terms of the beneficial entitlement to the property, it is necessary to decide whether the parties are *joint tenants* or *tenants in common*. Traditionally for a joint tenancy to exist the four unities must exist, i.e. unity of possession, title, time and interest. In that Gerald, Harry, James,

Kitty and Leslie acquire their rights by way of the 2000 conveyance this implies unity of title and time. They appear to have interests that are the same in extent, nature and duration and possession. Consequently the unities appear to be present, but this is not conclusive of a joint tenancy. It is only if one of the unities is missing that it can be concluded that a tenancy in common has been created. In that the conveyance provided that the parties were "joint tenants in law and equity" this will often be conclusive as to the creation of a joint tenancy. The fact that the parties have provided the purchase money in equal shares is also consistent with a joint tenancy. Nevertheless, the parties bought the property hoping that its value would increase and this may indicate a partnership venture, i.e. a common venture with a view to profit. As the *ius accrescendi* (right of survivorship) has no place in business this may indicate a tenancy in common. However, this is only an equitable presumption and will bow to the evidence to the contrary in the conveyance with the conclusion that the parties are joint tenants in equity.

The effect of Kitty's death in 2001 is that the legal estate will now be held by Gerald, Harry, James and Leslie as trustees. As the legal estate is held on a joint tenancy, the survivorship principle operates. In relation to the beneficial interests, again survivorship operates as the parties are joint tenants. The remaining parties (Gerald, Harry, James and Leslie) automatically absorb Kitty's "interest" in the property.

When Harry purchases James' share, this has no effect on the legal estate and James remains a trustee. The effect on the joint tenancy in equity is that severance takes place by way of the alienation of James' share to Harry. The unities of title and time are destroyed and, consequently, Harry holds a one-quarter share on a tenancy in common and the remaining three-quarters are still held on a joint-tenancy for Gerald, Harry and Leslie.

When Harry dies in 2005, the survivorship principle operates in respect of the legal estate and Gerald and James now hold the legal estate as trustees for the benefit of Gerald and Leslie as to three-quarters on a joint tenancy (Harry having lost his potential share by way of survivorship). The other one-quarter share on a tenancy in common which was held by Harry will now pass by virtue of his will to be held by his executor (James) for the benefit of his estate, the survivorship principle not operating in respect of a tenancy in common.

When Leslie orally agrees to purchase Gerald's interest in the property for £75,000 this has no effect on the legal estate. It does, however, raise issues as to whether this can amount to a severance of the joint tenancy in equity. In that the agreement is oral, there cannot be a valid contract to transfer the share and, therefore, it cannot be treated as alienation. Similarly the oral agreement does not comply with s.36(2) of the **LPA** which provides that severance can occur by written notice. The beneficial joint tenancy might be severed under the head of course of dealing between the joint tenants. In *Burgess v Rawnsley*, it was held that an oral agreement, in circumstances which clearly indicated that the parties treated themselves as having a share, amounted to a severance. Consequently the joint tenancy as to the three-quarters between Gerald and Leslie would appear to be severed.

The final position would appear to be that the legal estate is held by Gerald and James for the benefit of the estate of Harry's as to one-quarter, and three-eighths for Gerald and three-eighths for Leslie.

# Easements

## 11

## INTRODUCTION

An easement is a right annexed to land either to use (a positive easement) or, less usually, to restrict the use of (a negative easement), the land of another. The term derives from the Old French term "aisement" and means something that makes the enjoyment of land easier. An easement must confer a benefit on land (the dominant tenement) and burden other land (the servient tenement). It is often said that the categories of easement are never closed and that new rights might be admitted into the class as appropriate. The types of easement that can exist are, therefore, varied and include such rights as to use a neighbour's lavatory, to use a neighbour's washing line, to mix manure on a neighbour's land, to affix an advertising hoarding to a neighbour's building and to nail trees to an neighbour's wall. The major examples, however, are a right of way, a right of support and a right to light.

### Not to be Confused with
#### Profits a prendre

These offer the right to enter another's land and take something from the land which is naturally there (e.g. crops, timber, fish and animals). There is no need for a dominant tenement here as a profit can exist in gross. An easement offers no right to remove something from the land.

#### Licences

These are mere permissions to do something on the servient land. This might be gratuitous (i.e. without consideration) or contractual. It is never an interest in land, there is no need for a dominant tenement and it cannot bind third parties. The rights that can be the subject of a licence are, however, much wider than those captured by the law of easements.

#### Restrictive covenants

These are agreements to restrict the use of land for the benefit of other land. Freehold covenants are equitable interests only, cannot be acquired by long user and cover a wider range of restrictions than those subject to the few negative easements that can exist.

### Natural rights

These, unlike easements, emerge automatically from nature and do not depend upon another's grant. For example, a right to water flowing naturally through a defined channel.

### Public rights

These are exercisable by the general public (e.g. a public right of way under the Countryside and Rights of Way Act 2000). There is no need for any dominant tenement and the rights are never the subject of a grant.

### Rights under the Access to Neighbouring Land Act 1992

This makes provision to enable a person to gain access to neighbouring land in order to carry out works which are reasonably necessary for the preservation of his own land. This allows the court to grant an "access order" for the purpose of effecting repairs. This is not an easement, but is more than a mere licence. It is a statutory right effected by court order. The order can be made subject to such terms and conditions as the court deems necessary to avoid loss, damage and inconvenience to the landowner. In unregistered land, an access order can be registered in the register of writs and orders affecting land. In registered land, the **Land Registration Act 2002** allows it to be protected by entry of a notice.

## STATUS

### Legal or Equitable?
An easement is one of the five interests listed in s.1(2) of the **Law of Property Act 1925** as having the capacity to exist as a legal interest. Whether it is legal or not depends upon its duration (a legal easement must be timed to reflect either a freehold or leasehold) and the manner of its creation. If it is created by deed, it will be legal: s.52. If it fails to satisfy either of these conditions, it will necessarily be an equitable easement.

### Benefit of an Existing Easement
The benefit of an existing easement (whether legal or equitable) will automatically pass to a purchaser of the dominant land by virtue of s.62 of the **LPA**. This is primarily a word saving provision which entails that the seller does not have

to assign the benefit expressly on each conveyance. As to whether the burden of an existing easement will pass on the sale of the servient land, this issue will turn upon whether the easement is legal or equitable and whether the land is unregistered or registered.

## INGREDIENTS

It was laid down in *Re Ellenborough Park* (1956) that there are four essential characteristics of an easement:

- there must be a dominant and servient tenement;
- the right must benefit the dominant land;
- there must be diversity of ownership or, at the least, occupation; and
- the right must be capable of lying in grant.

### Two Tenements

There must be both a dominant tenement and a servient tenement which means, essentially, that there must be one piece of land which carries the benefit and another which carries the burden. An easement cannot, therefore, exist in gross independent of ownership in land. In *London & Blenheim Estates v Ladbroke Retail Parks* (1994), there was no easement because the potential servient tenement had been transferred before the dominant tenement had been acquired. The grantor and grantee of the "easement" did not, at the time of the grant, hold the respective estates in the dominant and servient tenements. A right given to a person with no dominant land will usually fall to be classified as a licence.

### Accommodating the Dominant Tenement

The right must accommodate (i.e. benefit) the dominant tenement or a business carried out there. This means that the right "must have some natural connection with the estate as being for its benefit" (*Bailey v Stephens* (1862)). The test, simply put, is whether the right makes the dominant tenement a better and more convenient property. A right to free tickets at a neighbouring football ground might increase the value of the dominant land, but it has nothing to do with the use of the land and cannot be an easement. In contrast, a right that improves the general utility of the dominant tenement, say, by giving a means of access or light clearly accommodates the land.

#### Trade

In *Moody v Steggles* (1879), it was held that the right to fix an advertising sign to an adjoining property accommodated the business of a public house operating on the dominant land. It has to advertise the business, however, and not merely some product sold there. Hence, a sign adjacent to a supermarket that simply states "Drink Milk" is unlikely to bestow a sufficiently direct benefit on the business conducted on the dominant land. It should, seemingly, be different if the sign read "Buy your Milk at our Supermarket". In *Hill v Tupper* (1863), the tenant of land adjacent to a canal claimed as an easement the exclusive right to operate pleasure boats on the canal. This argument was rejected because the right was of benefit only to Mr Hill's pocket and not his land. It was merely a licence. It could not, moreover, be said to benefit a business carried on the dominant tenement because his business was instead carried out on the servient tenement (i.e. the canal).

### Geographic proximity

Although the dominant and servient tenements need not be adjoining, they must be sufficiently proximate for a practical benefit to be conferred: *Pugh v Savage* (1970). As Byles J. put it, "You cannot have a right of way over land in Kent appurtenant to an estate in London" (*Bailey v Stephens* (1862)). It might, however, be possible to have an easement to run horses on gallops at Epsom even though the business of training race horses is situated in Glasgow.

### The Dominant and Servient Tenement must not be Owned and Occupied by the Same Person

It is not possible to have an easement over one's own land because an easement is a right exercisable over the soil of another. Rights exercised by an owner over his own land are sometimes known as quasi-easements (see below). It is possible, however, that a landlord can acquire an easement over his tenant's land (and vice versa) because there is no common occupation: *Borman v Griffith* (1930). It is also permissible to have an easement where the servient tenement is owned by, say, husband and wife and the dominant tenement is owned by the husband alone: *Sweet v Sommer* (2004).

### The Easement must be Capable of Forming the Subject Matter of a Grant

This entails that:

### There must be a capable grantor and grantee

A problem can arise where a tenement is owned by a corporation which does not have the power to grant or receive easements. In such cases, the easement must fail. In *Sweet v Sommer* (2004), the alleged servient tenement was jointly owned by a husband and wife and a purported grant of a right of way by the husband was held to be invalid because he alone was not a capable grantor.

### The right must be sufficiently definite that it could be granted by deed (i.e. it must be known what right is granted)

A vague or inexact right cannot exist as an easement. There is, therefore, no easement of privacy: *Browne v Flower* (1911). Similarly, there is not a right to a view nor a right to the general flow of air (not being in a defined channel) over land: *Harris v De Pinna* (1886);

### The right must be within the general nature of rights capable of existing as easements

The list of easements is not closed and, as admitted in *Dyce v Hay* (1852), must accommodate societal change. For example, there are relatively new easements to park a car (*Moncrieff v Jamieson* (2007)) and to use an airfield (*Dowty Boulton Paul Ltd v Wolverhampton Corp (No. 2)* (1976)). Nevertheless, as Lord Brougham put it in *Keppel v Bailey* (1834), "incidents of a novel kind cannot be devised at the fancy or caprice of any owner".

### Rights unlikely to qualify as easements

Although the right may exhibit the other characteristics set out in *Re Ellenborough Park* (1968), it is likely that a new easement will not be recognised where:

- it involves expenditure by the servient owner: *Rance v Elvin* (1983). The only exception to this rule is the easement to require the servient owner to fence his land: *Crow v Wood* (1971);
- it is a negative right, i.e. a right to stop a neighbour from doing something on his own land. In *Phipps v Pears* (1965), it was held that there could be no easement affording protection from the weather. This was because it was a negative right;
- it involves exclusive or joint user. The approach is simple: an easement is a right over someone else's land and, if the right amounts to exclusive or joint use, it contradicts the ownership rights of the servient owner: *Copeland v Greenhalf* (1952). There, the storage and repair of vehicles on a narrow strip of land was so excessive that it excluded the servient owner from the land and went well beyond the normal idea of an easement. Similarly, in *Grigsby v Melville* (1972) the right to store goods in a cellar was rejected as an easement because it would give an exclusive right of

use. In *Hanina v Morland* (2000), the claim to the exclusive use of a roof terrace could not lie in grant and was not an easement. These cases amount to a positive claim to legal possession of the servient tenement. If the exclusive use is not permanent, however, the court must decide which side of the line the right falls. Although a right to use a lavatory will involve an element of exclusive use, in *Miller v Emcer* (1956) it was upheld as an easement. In *Ward v Kirkland* (1969) a right to enter on the servient land in order to repair a wall on the dominant land was an easement as it involved only a trace of exclusive use by the dominant owner. These rights are clearly of a non-possessory nature.

### Parking problems?

Problems can arise, however, with the right to park a car. If the right is to park anywhere on the servient land, then that can properly be regarded as an easement. It is merely a claim to use and not to possession. If, however, it is a right to park in a particular parking bay then, it is arguable, that might be too extensive to amount to an easement because of the total ouster of the servient owner.

### Moncrieff v Jamieson

The vexed question of whether and, if so, when a right to park a motor vehicle can constitute an easement preoccupied the House of Lords in *Moncrieff v Jamieson* (2007). There an express grant of a right of way (making no reference to parking rights) was held to include an implied right to park because the circumstances demanded such an implication. The House of Lords, moreover, considered the "ouster principle", but did not speak with one voice. The majority preferred not to speculate when the principle would prevent an easement to park from arising. Lord Scott, however, had no such inhibitions. He saw no objection whatsoever with an easement to park in an allocated bay. There remained other uses to which the servient tenement could potentially be put which would reinforce the servient owner's possession and control. For example, the servient owner could build above or under the parking area and place advertising hoardings on the adjacent walls. Whether Lord Scott's approach will be followed is highly debatable.

............................................................................................

## EASEMENT CREATION

A basic principle is that all easements will have their origin in a grant and most methods of acquisition are traceable to a grant whether real or fictitious. The following methods of acquisition exist.

## Statute

Easements may be granted by local Acts of Parliament, for example, giving a right of support to a canal constructed under statute or by general Act of Parliament, giving rights in respect of cables, gas pipes, sewers, etc.

**Figure 12: Grants and Reservations**

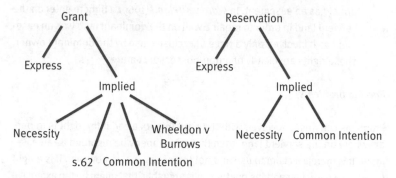

## Express Grant or Reservation

A common way of creating easements is by way of express grant or reservation. A grant occurs where the servient owner grants a right over his own land, e.g. X sells off Blueacre to Y and in the conveyance grants to Y a right of way over Blackacre which is land retained by X. Conversely, a reservation arises where a vendor wishes to reserve an easement over the land sold, e.g. X sells off Blueacre to Y, but in the conveyance to Y reserves for himself a right of way over Blueacre for the benefit of Blackacre. The extent of the right is, of course, dependent upon how it is described in the conveyance. No special words are necessary as long as the intention is clear.

## Implied Grant or Reservation

At this point, grants and reservations are treated very differently. Implied grants are based upon the notion that there shall be no derogation from grant and are more common than implied reservations: *Peckham v Ellison* (1998). This is because the onus is on the vendor to reserve an easement expressly in the conveyance: *Re Webb's Lease* (1951). It is important to appreciate that a reservation will be implied only in relation to an easement of necessity or a common intention.

## Easements of Necessity

These are implied only in what are called land locked close situations where it is necessary to imply an easement so that the dominant owner can gain access to the dominant tenement: *Pinnington v Gallard* (1853). For example, X sells part of his land to Y. There is no means of access to the part bought except over the land retained by X. In these circumstances, if the conveyance is silent, a right of way will be impliedly granted to Y because of necessity. Alternatively, if X sells off part of his land to Y and X cannot gain access to the part he retains without crossing the land sold to Y, a reservation will then be implied. In *Manjang V Drammeh* (1991), three conditions for the existence of an easement of necessity were set out:

- there must have been a common owner of two plots;
- access between the plots and the highway can be achieved only via the other plot. If the necessity ceases so does the easement: *Donaldson v Smith* (2006);
- one of the plots was sold without any express grant or reservation of a right of way. It is to be appreciated that an easement of necessity will not be implied if it is excluded by the clearly expressed contrary intentions of the parties: *Hillman v Rogers* (1997).

### Bipartite and tripartite models

Prior to the Court of Appeal decision in *Adealon International Property Ltd v Merton LBC* (2007), it was thought that the dominant land had to be entirely surrounded by the servient land. This is the traditional bipartite model in which easements of necessity are implied. This is no longer a hard and fast rule as the appellate court recognised that an easement of necessity could arise in a tripartite scenario. There the vendor retained land which was cut off from the highway. One of the bordering plots of land was, however, owned by a third party. The issue which arose was whether the adjoining land of a stranger to the grant prevented an easement of necessity arising. The Court of Appeal held that the existence of third party land was fatal as regards a reservation of necessity. It was up to the vendor to expressly reserve a right of way and it had nothing to do with non-derogation from grant. The appellate court did, however, make the point that the adjoining land of a third party would not prevent the grant of an easement of necessity.

### More than convenience

The implication hinges on necessity and not mere convenience. In *Manjang v Drammeh* (1991), the Privy Council confirmed that an available access by water, even though less convenient than access across land, was sufficient to negative any implication of a right of way of necessity. In *Sweet v Sommer* (2004), however, the possibility of demolishing a shed in order to gain alternative access did not prevent an easement of necessity being implied.

## Common Intention Easements

These are implied to give effect to the common intention of the parties. In *Stafford v Lee* (1993), a right of way for construction vehicles while a house was being built was implied as it was the common intention of the parties that the house was to be erected on the dominant land. In *Wong v Beaumont Property Trust* (1965), the landlord let cellars to the tenant who covenanted to use them as a restaurant and to comply with health regulations. It later transpired that, in order to comply with the regulations, the tenant had to install an effective ventilation system. This could occur only if the tenant was allowed to run ventilation shafts up the side of the landlord's wall. The landlord refused the tenant's request, but the court held that the tenant had an implied easement to affix the shafts. In appropriate circumstances, a common intention easement can be impliedly reserved.

### Conditions

In *Davies v Bramwell* (2007), a right of way was upheld as a common intention easement. In doing so, the court advocated a two stage approach:

* the court must find a common intention that the dominant land should be used in some particular or definite manner; and
* the grant or reservation must be required in order to give effect to that intention.

## The Rule in Wheeldon v Burrows

The rule is that, when a vendor sells off part of his land, the purchaser will acquire through implication:

> "all those continuous and apparent . . . quasi-easements . . . which are necessary to the reasonable enjoyment of the property granted, and which have been and are at the time of the grant used by the owners of the entirety for the benefit of the part granted" (per Thesiger L.J.).

The rule is based upon the rule against derogation from grant. The rule, therefore, concerns so called quasi-easements (rights which the owner previously exercised over the land he retains for the benefit of the part he has disposed of). These rights can be elevated to proper easements (either legal or equitable) on the dealing with the quasi-dominant tenement. For example, in *McAdams Homes Ltd v Robinson* (2004) an easement of drainage was created under this rule.

### Conditions

The conditions necessary for a *Wheeldon v Burrows* (1879) easement to be implied are:

- there must be common ownership and occupation of the entirety of the land prior to the rule being triggered. One without the other is insufficient: *Kent v Kavanagh* (2006);
- the quasi-dominant tenement must be dealt with (e.g. sold, leased, acquired by will or subject to a contract to sell). Hence, the rule only applies to implied grants and cannot be relied upon to justify an implied reservation. The rule also applies if the common owner deals with both parts simultaneously: *Swansborough v Coventry* (1832). In *Donaldson v Smith* (2006), the two transactions were four months apart and yet this difference in time did not destroy the "simultaneity" of the two appoint-ments. They were still to be regarded as in effect part and parcel of a single transaction. The effect is as if the owner had sold the dominant tenement and retained the rest: *Schwann v Cotton* (1916);
- the right must be continuous and apparent. Continuous appears to mean permanent, i.e. the right must be regularly exercised. Apparent implies that there must be a discernible trace of the right on the land itself which, at the very least, must be one that would be revealed by a careful inspec-tion of the land. A rough track was sufficient in *Hansford v Jago* (1921). Other examples would include water flowing through visible pipes, win-dows enjoying light or a defined passageway;
- the right must be reasonably necessary to the enjoyment of the land. It has never been authoritatively established whether this reference is an alternative to the right being "continuous and apparent" or whether both conditions must be satisfied. The traditional view appears to be that both must be satisfied: *Wheeler v JJ Saunders* (1995). There a right of way was not implied because, as an alternative access to the property existed, it was not deemed necessary for the reasonable enjoyment of the land;
- the right must have been used by the common owner up to the time of the grant, i.e. when the quasi-dominant tenement was dealt with. *Wheeldon v Burrows* does not operate to resurrect past rights; and
- there must be no express contracting out of the operation of the rule.

### Section 62 of the LPA 1925
Section 62 states that, subject to a contrary intention expressed in the convey-ance, every conveyance of land passes all privileges, easements, rights and advantages appertaining or reputed to appertain to the land or part of it. This

general word saving provision can have unexpected consequences. It not only transmits the benefit of existing easements to a purchaser of the dominant tenement, but it can also create new legal easements from, say, what was previously a revocable licence. In *Wright v Macadam* (1940), the permissive right to use a coal shed passed as a legal easement under s.62 on the grant of a new lease. An implied grant (but never a reservation) can arise under s.62 where:

- there is a conveyance of the dominant tenement. The term "conveyance" is defined in s.205 of the **LPA** and includes such transactions as a mortgage, lease and assent. It does not include a will, gift or contract. Seemingly, it also does not include oral tenancy: *Borman v Griffith* (1930);
- prior to the conveyance, there was common ownership of the dominant tenements, but diversity of occupation: see Lord Wilberforce in *Sovmots Investments v Secretary of State* (1979). Some judges have, however, concluded that the requirement of diversity of occupation gives way when the right is continuous and apparent (see Peter Gibson L.J. in *P&S Platt Ltd v Crouch* (2003)). This is, therefore, an area of some uncertainty and it is better to canvas both approaches. Nevertheless, an insistence upon diversity of occupation is attractive in that it keeps s.62 and the rule in *Wheeldon v Burrows* apart in mutually exclusive spheres. This is appealing both in terms of logic and symmetry and is line with the approach adopted by the House of Lords in the *Sovmots* case and more recently approved by Chadwick L.J. in *Kent v Kavanagh* (2006); and
- there is no contrary intention specified in the conveyance or contract which precedes it;
- the right is one which existed at the time of the conveyance and is not a spent or past right.

## Prescription

### ▌ DEFINITION CHECKPOINT

Prescription relates to easements acquired by presumed grant, i.e. where the law presumes from long enjoyment that the right had its lawful origin in a grant. A prescriptive right may be acquired either at common law, under the doctrine of lost modern grant or by virtue of the **Prescription Act 1832**. In each case certain common criteria must be established.

### *The use must be "as of right"*

This is explained in the maxim *nec per vim, nec clam, nec precario* which requires that the right has not been obtained by force or coercion, and that it is not secretive: *Union Lighterage Co v London Graving* (1902). The use, moreover, must not be permissive in nature. For example, in *Kent v Kavanagh* (2006) a claim to a prescriptive easement to use a path failed because a previous owner had asked permission to use the path.

### The user must be continuous

User can be by successive owners of the dominant tenement: *Davis v Whitby* (1974). A right of way used precariously (blocked at irregular intervals) cannot, however, develop into an easement: *Goldsmith v Burrow Construction Co Ltd* (1987).

### The user must be by or on behalf of a fee simple owner against a fee simple owner

If a tenant acquires an easement against a third party he acquires it on behalf of the fee simple estate. If a tenant occupies the servient tenement, an easement cannot be acquired against it. If the user began against a fee simple owner, however, it does not make it invalid for prescriptive purposes if the land is later leased. The general rule is that easements be prescribed for by one tenant against another tenant of the same landlord: *Simmons v Dobson* (1991).

### The user must not be prohibited by statute or contrary to public policy

This covers cases when the grant would involve using the land in a prohibited way. This would be an unlawful grant and incapable of vesting any right in the grantee: *Bakewell Management Ltd v Brandwood* (2004). Accordingly, if the landowner has the power lawfully to make an express grant of an easement, it follows that it is a right that can also be acquired by prescription.

## Common Law Prescription

At common law, a grant was presumed if enjoyment dated from time immemorial (1189). To overcome obvious evidential difficulties, the courts adopted the stance that, if 20 years' user could be shown, it would be assumed that the right had been enjoyed since 1189. This presumption will be rebutted if it could be shown that, at any time since 1189, the right could not have existed. For example, a claim to a right of light to a building erected after that date would fail. Similarly, if it could be shown that the dominant and servient tenements had been in common ownership since 1189, the presumption would not operate.

## Lost Modern Grant

A mechanism to avoid the rigors of the common law rule was developed by the courts under the fiction of lost modern grant. If a claimant can show actual enjoyment for a period of 20 years, the court is prepared to pretend that there was once a grant that has now been lost: *Dalton v Angus* (1881). As the grant never actually existed, there is no need to furnish the court with any particulars of it. The claim may, however, be defeated if proof is given that during the entire period since user started there has been no person capable of granting easements: *Tehidy Minerals Ltd v Norman* (1971). Although most claims will now fall under the **Prescription Act 1832**, the doctrine of lost modern grant is still invoked.

### The Prescription Act 1832

The object of this Act was to simplify the method of acquisition of easements by prescription, but it was a poor attempt. The Act has been subjected to repeated criticism and it is amazing that it still forms a central part of modern property law. The Act draws a basic distinction between easements of light and other types of easement.

#### *Easements other than light*

Section 2 provides that an easement can be claimed where it is "actually enjoyed by any person claiming right thereto without interruption for the full period of 20 years". It cannot be defeated by showing that the user began after 1189. It may, however, be defeated in other ways, for example, if it was secretive, permissive or forcible user. The law changes as regards uninterrupted actual enjoyment for 40 years. This extended user makes the right absolute and indefeasible unless enjoyed by express consent given by deed or writing.

#### *Easements of light*

Section 3 provides that, where a right of light has been actually enjoyed for a full period of 20 years without interruption, the right becomes absolute and indefeasible, unless enjoyed by written consent or agreement. Oral permission will not defeat this claim. The following points emerge:

- the amount of light that a building is entitled to is that which is required for any ordinary purpose for which the building has been constructed or adapted: *Colls v Home and Colonial Stores Ltd* (1904);
- an interruption of a right of light may be effected by erecting an obstruction, or alternatively by registration of a local land charge to have effect as an obstruction under the Rights of Light Act 1959; and
- a tenant may acquire an easement of light against another tenant of the same landlord. This is an exception to the rule that prescription can operate only between freeholders.

# EXTINGUISHMENT OF EASEMENTS

## Abandonment
This can occur by:

- express release. A deed is required at common law, but equity will assist a servient owner who, relying on an agreement to release, acts to his prejudice. This will give rise to an estoppel which will prevent the other party denying the non-existence of the easement; or,
- implied release (abandonment). An intention to abandon must be shown, but non-user alone is inconclusive.

### Inferred abandonment

This can arise where the dominant owner manifests an intention to abandon the right and makes clear that neither he nor his successors will thereafter make use of the right. Abandonment is not, however, lightly to be inferred. Non-user for 175 years of a right of way granted in 1818 did not of itself indicate an intention to abandon in *Benn v Hardinge* (1992). In *CDC2020 Plc v Ferreira* (2005), a right of way to reach garages was not abandoned even though the garages were demolished and replaced by a basement car park. Lloyd L.J. considered whether the dominant owner had made it clear that it was his firm intention, at the time of the construction works, to abandon and never to resume the right of way. He concluded, "demolition of the garages, with or without failure to use the way, even for a long period, would not be enough". The burden of showing an inference of abandonment was not discharged.

### Practical impossibility

A change of circumstances might also cause an easement to be extinguished. If there is no longer any practical possibility of the easement ever again benefiting the dominant tenement in the manner originally contemplated, the easement will lapse: *Huckvale v Aegean Hotels Ltd* (1989). In *National Guarantee Manure Co v Donald* (1859), a right to a defined supply of water to a canal ceased to exist when the canal was later filled up and turned into a railway. Similarly, in *Cook v Bath Corp* (1868), the back door of a house had been bricked up for 40 years. An easement over the passageway to which the back door gave access was held to have been abandoned.

## Unity of Ownership and Possession
Where the fee simple of both tenements becomes vested in the same owner, the easement will be extinguished. It is not possible to have an easement over

one's own land. The easement will not be revived on any subsequent sale of one of the tenements.

## Statute

An easement may be extinguished either expressly or by implication by Act of Parliament, for example, under the Commons Registration Act 1965.

## Change of Use and Increased Burden

In *McAdams Homes Ltd v Robinson* (2004), the dominant land was redeveloped with the result that a former bakery was demolished and replaced by two detached houses. An existing easement of drainage was interrupted by the owner of the servient land. The Court of Appeal held that the easement had been lost because the development represented a radical change in the character or a change in the identity of the site and amounted to a substantial increase or alteration in the burden on the servient land.

### Revision Checklist

You should now know and understand:

- what an easement is and how it differs from other rights;
- the *Re Ellenborough Park* criteria;
- how easements may be created expressly or arise through implication;
- the rules as to acquiring easements by prescription;
- the ways in which easements may be brought to an end.

## QUESTION AND ANSWER

### Question

Clive owns and occupies the adjoining properties known as "The House" and "The Field". Clive allows his friend, Norma, to rent "The House". When living in "The House", Clive had always used a shortcut across "The Field" in order to get to the nearby village. Subsequently, Clive gives Norma permission to park anywhere on "The Field", whenever she likes. Some months later, Norma buys the freehold of "The House" from Clive. Clive now wishes to prevent Norma from crossing over and parking on the grounds of "The Field". "The House" also has the benefit of a legal easement of light from the adjoining Mondo Villas, owned by Mrs Hughes. Construction work is to begin on Mondo Villas that will interrupt this flow of light.

With reference to *Wheeldon v Burrows* and s.62 of the Law of Property Act 1925, advise the parties.

## Advice and the Answer

The answer should open with a consideration whether these rights (i.e. a right to cross land and a right to park on land) can exist as easements. It is quite clear that the basic ingredients of an easement as set out in *Re Ellenborough Park* are satisfied here. Some reference, however, should be made to easements to park and the problems that might arise if the right is limited to a particular parking bay. Even after *Moncrieff v Jamieson*, it remains unclear when a parking right will be disqualified because of the ouster principle. Nevertheless, there is no problem with the ability to park anywhere in a field.

As to the benefit of the existing easement giving a right of light over Mondo Villas, this will pass automatically under s.62 of the **LPA** to a purchaser of "The House". This avoids the need to expressly assign the benefit on each sale of the dominant land. All that is necessary is that there is a conveyance (i.e. a formal document of transfer) and no contrary intention demonstrated. When Norma rents "The House" it is unclear whether she does so under a lease created by deed or under some other informal arrangement. At the stage she takes her lease, therefore, it is unclear whether she would have the benefit of the existing easement passed to her (for the duration of the lease) by virtue of s.62. Put simply, you do not know whether there was a conveyance at this stage. At the latest, Norma will, however, acquire the benefit on her purchase of the freehold estate. Such a purchase would require a conveyance.

The more difficult issue here is to do with whether Clive has granted new easements in favour of Norma. There is no question of any reservations in favour of Clive here. As neither of the rights were expressly granted nor is there any case for prescription, it is necessary to consider whether they have been created by implication. There are four ways in which this can occur: necessity, common intention, under the rule in *Wheeldon v Burrows* and by virtue of s.62 of the **LPA**. The dominant tenement is not land locked so there is no scope for an easement of necessity. In addition, there was no mutual understanding between the parties as to the use of the dominant land which could only be achieved by the implication of a common intention easement. Hence, Norma will have to focus upon the rule in *Wheeldon v Burrows* and the operation of s.62 of the **LPA**.

As regards *Wheeldon v Burrows*, a number of factors have to be established. First, that prior to the lease to Norma, the dominant ("The House") and servient ("The Field") tenements were owned and occupied by the same person. Clive owned and occupied both until Norma came on the scene. Secondly, it is the quasi-dominant tenement that must be leased to Norma. The lease is of "The House" so there is no problem here. Thirdly, the right must have been enjoyed by Clive until the time of the lease. It seems that he used the shortcut over his own land to the village up until Norma took the tenancy. Fourthly, the right must be continuous and apparent. "Continuous" refers to the shortcut being more than a temporary convenience and being of a permanent nature. "Apparent" entails that there is some trace of the exercise of the shortcut from. Both are likely to be satisfied on the present facts. Fifthly, the right must be reasonably necessary to the enjoyment of the quasi-dominant land. Following *Wheeler v JJ Saunders*, Norma will have to establish this fifth element in addition to (and not as an alternative to) the fourth element. The right of way claimed here will, seemingly, be reasonably necessary. Finally, there must be no express contracting out of the *Wheeldon v Burrows*. There is no suggestion that the lease excluded the operation of the rule. Hence, when Norma takes the lease, she will have implied a *Wheeldon v Burrows* easement concerning the right of way across "The Field".

Further observations should be made as to the status and duration of Norma's right of way when she takes the lease. The *Wheeldon v Burrows* easement will last for as long as the lease. Accordingly, if she did not subsequently purchase the freehold, the easement would be extinguished when the lease ended and Clive resumed occupation of "the House". It is to be recalled that you cannot have an easement over your own land. As to whether the implied right of way is legal or equitable, this turns upon how the lease to Norma was created. If it was created by deed, the *Wheeldon v Burrows* easement would be legal (s.52 of the **LPA**). If it was created in writing or orally, the easement must necessarily be equitable due to the absence of a deed.

In relation to s.62 of the **LPA**, this will become relevant when Norma purchases the freehold of "the House". If it operates it will raise the status of the right of way to a legal easement attached to the freehold estate. Perhaps more surprisingly, it will elevate what was previously a revocable licence to park a car into an easement attached to the freehold estate (*Wright v Macadam*). In order for s.62 to operate a number of factors must be present. There must be common ownership, but diversity of occupation before the sale of the dominant tenement to Norma (*Sovmots Investments Ltd v Secretary of State*).

This is clearly satisfied on the present facts as prior to the sale Clive was the freeholder of both plots with Norma occupying the dominant land ("The House") and Clive occupying the servient land ("The Field"). The rights claimed must be "live" rights in that they must be exercised by Norma up to the time of the sale. There must also be a conveyance (i.e. a formal transfer of the land) into which the easements can be implied. A formal transfer will be necessary in order to transfer the freehold estate to Norma. Finally, there must be no contracting out of the operation of s.62. There is no suggestion that this has occurred. Hence, s.62 will bite on the present facts and Norma will acquire the right of way and the right to park as legal easements. As mentioned, the conveyance to her will also pass the benefit of the existing right to light over Mondo Villas.

# Mortgages

## 12

## INTRODUCTION

A mortgage (whether legal or equitable) is essentially a pledge of land as security for the repayment of a loan. The person who borrows the money is known as the mortgagor and the lender is the mortgagee. The borrower retains legal title to the land and will remain in occupation of the property. The borrower has a right of redemption (i.e. to pay off the mortgage) at any time after the contractual date for redemption (see below). The borrower's rights under the mortgage are for simplicity often described as the mortgagor's equity of redemption. The lender is a secured creditor and acquires a property interest in the land. This is a much stronger position than with an unsecured creditor. For example, on the mortgagor's bankruptcy the mortgagee's claim will prevail against other creditors. If the borrower defaults on, say, repayment, the lender has an extensive array of remedies which can be employed. The main remedy of the mortgagee is the power to sell the mortgaged property.

## CREATION OF MORTGAGES

### Legal Mortgages of Unregistered Land
*Freehold*

By virtue of s.85(1) of the **Law of Property Act 1925** legal mortgages of an unregistered freehold estate may still be created in one of two ways:

- by a demise for a term of years absolute, subject to a provision for redemption. Any attempt to create a mortgage by conveyance of the freehold estate is to take effect as a lease for 3,000 years: s.85(2); or
- by a charge by deed expressed to be by way of legal mortgage. The mortgagee has all the same protection, powers and remedies as if the mortgage had been created by the grant of a term of years: s.87(1) of the **LPA**.

*Leasehold*

By virtue of s.86(1) of the **LPA**, legal mortgages of an unregistered leasehold estate can be created in two ways:

- by granting a sub-lease of a term of years absolute to the mortgagee subject to a provision for redemption; or
- by a charge by deed expressed to be by way of legal mortgage.

## Legal Mortgages of Registered Land

A legal mortgage of registered land can now be created only by a charge expressed to be by way of legal mortgage: s.23(1)(a) of the **Land Registration Act 2002**. The mortgage, moreover, only becomes legal once it is registered as a charge at the Land Registry. Whether it is the freehold or leasehold estate that is the subject of the mortgage, it is no longer possible to have a mortgage by demise or sub-demise of registered land. This shift has occurred because a legal charge has some practical advantages over the other types of mortgage:

- it is convenient, less cumbersome and less expensive;
- it is easier to understand and explain to a purchaser;
- it does not infringe a provision (in a lease) against subletting.

## Equitable Mortgages

Equitable mortgages are rare, but will arise where there is insufficient formality to create a legal mortgage, i.e. in the absence of a deed. An equitable mortgage will be created if, for example, the mortgage is merely in writing. If, however, it is in writing, and satisfies the other conditions of s.2 of the **Law of Property (Miscellaneous Provisions) Act 1989** (i.e. it is signed by both parties and contains all the express terms), it might amount to a valid contract to create a legal mortgage. In such circumstances the court may award specific performance of the contract and direct that a deed be executed to overcome the lack of formality. If there is no writing whatsoever then it cannot even exist as an equitable mortgage: s.53(1)(a) of the **LPA**.

### *Mortgage of an equitable interest*

A mortgage of an equitable interest, regardless of how it is created, must necessarily be equitable. For example, the mortgage of a life estate or a beneficial interest under a trust of land or strict settlement must, therefore, be an equitable mortgage. The lender will acquire the entire equitable interest, subject to a proviso for reassignment on full payment of the loan.

# RIGHTS OF THE BORROWER

## The Right to Redeem

Once a mortgage has been created, there will normally be a contractual date set for repayment of the loan. This is known as "the date for legal redemption". The date is often set six months from the date of the loan. Until this time, the borrower cannot redeem (without the consent of the lender) nor can the lender exercise some of its key remedies, e.g. sale or the appointment of a receiver. At common law, if the money was not paid on the precise date, the property automatically vested in the mortgagee. This was a harsh and unfair rule and so equity intervened and created an equitable right to redeem, i.e. the mortgagor acquired the equitable right to redeem the property once the legal redemption date had passed. The right to redeem lasts until sale of the property or foreclosure of the mortgage. This should not be confused with the equity of redemption (shorthand for the entire interest of the borrower under the mortgage).

### *Is it a mortgage?*

Difficulties can arise, as in *Dutton v Davis* (2006), where one party argues that there was a conveyance of the freehold with an option to repurchase within a set time frame and the other party argues that in substance the transaction was a mortgage. As Lloyd L.J. put it, "That involves the proposition that the transaction, despite its appearance, was really a mortgage under which he has an equitable right of redemption". There, and although the agreement was framed in clear and unambiguous language, it was held in substance to be a mortgage transaction. This reflects the traditional approach echoed by Harman L.J. in *Grangeside Properties Ltd v Collingwoods Securities* (1964), "once a mortgage, always a mortgage and nothing but a mortgage . . .".

### *Clogs and fetters*

Any provision preventing a mortgagor from recovering the property after redemption is repugnant to the nature of the transaction and void. It is said that there can be "no clog or fetter on the right to redeem". A provision in a mortgage that stipulates that property shall belong to the mortgagee on the occurrence of some event is, thereby, ineffective. Similarly an option to purchase contained in a mortgage deed is void: *Samuel v Jarrah Timber* (1904). Such a provision contradicts the equitable right to redeem: *Jones v Morgan* (2001). If, however, the option is granted by the borrower in a separate and independent transaction, it can be upheld: *Reeve v Lisle* (1902).

## Modifications

The right to redeem may, however, be restricted or modified. A provision postponing the date of redemption may be valid provided that it does not make the equitable right to redeem of no value. In *Fairclough v Swan Brewery Co Ltd* (1912), a 17-year lease of a brewery was mortgaged on conditions that prevented its redemption until six weeks before the end of the term. This was held to make the equitable right to redeem illusory and therefore void. By way of contrast, in *Knightsbridge Estates Trust Ltd v Byrne* (1939) it was held that, in the context of a mortgage of the freehold estate, a clause postponing redemption for 40 years was valid. There it was significant that the parties were large commercial enterprises that had entered into a mutually enforceable agreement after being professionally advised. The key notion is that any postponement cannot be oppressive or unconscionable. Equity will not, however, rewrite a mortgage transaction simply because the postponement is unreasonable.

## Restraint of trade

A mortgage is subject to the common law rule that an agreement which operates as an unreasonable restraint of trade is void. For example, in *Esso Petroleum v Harper's Garage (Stourport) Ltd* (1968) an agreement which tied the borrower to selling only the products of the lender (sometimes called a solus agreement) for a period of 21 years was invalid. It appears that the court will uphold solus agreements that are limited to relatively short periods. In the *Esso Petroleum* case, a tie in for five years was upheld.

## Collateral advantages

Collateral advantages might be reserved in the mortgage in addition to the repayment of the loan and interest. These added or ancillary obligations (also including a "solus" agreement) are permitted providing that they are not unconscionable and do not constitute a clog on the right to redeem. In *Noakes v Rice* (1902), the mortgagor of a public house agreed that he would sell only the lender's beer for the duration of a 26-year lease. The collateral advantage was void because it was oppressive as it was to continue after redemption of the mortgage. In *Biggs v Hoddinott* (1898), however, the mortgage agreement provided that the mortgage could not be redeemed for five years and that, during this period, the borrower would sell only the lender's products. The collateral advantage was upheld as, unlike in the *Noakes* case, it was reasonable and fair. In *Cityland Holdings Ltd v Dabrah* (1968), however, a provision which entailed that the interest rate would rise to 57 per cent on any default in repayment (at a time when the national rate was seven per cent) was regarded as an unconscionable collateral advantage and held to be void.

### Sustaining collateral advantages

As a general rule any collateral advantage must cease when the mortgage is redeemed: *Bradley v Carritt* (1903). In *Kreglinger v New Patagonia Meat and Cold Storage Co Ltd* (1914), however, the House of Lords upheld a mortgage term which provided that, for a period of five years, the mortgagor could not sell any animal skins to anyone other than the mortgagee. Although the mortgage was paid off within three years, the collateral advantage was viewed as a distinct and independent agreement and, as such, it was capable of continuing in force after the mortgage had been redeemed. It was a bona fide business deal between the parties.

## The Right to Grant Leases

By virtue of s.99 of the **LPA,** the mortgagor in possession can grant certain leases that will be binding on the mortgage lender. This power can, however, be excluded in the mortgage agreement and this is common practice. A mortgagee will not be bound by an unauthorised lease and the lender has an unqualified right to take possession as against an unauthorised tenant.

## The Right to be Protected from Unfair Agreements

This section focuses upon the freely negotiated terms of the agreement and the circumstances in which they can be overridden. Although the Unfair Contract Terms Act 1977 does not apply to mortgages, two other pieces of legislation enjoy the potential to apply to land mortgages: the Financial Services and Markets Act 2000 and, to a lesser extent, the Consumer Credit Act 2006.

### The 2000 Act

A new code of conduct for mortgage lenders requires "responsible lending". This code is to be found in the Financial Services Authority Handbook. The **Financial Services and Markets Act** ensures that mortgage lenders do not levy exorbitant charges on their customers and adds transparency to the charges made. The Act imposes a wide range of possible sanctions for breach of its provisions. The 2000 Act catches the vast majority of mortgage transactions. It extends to financial services provided by (amongst others) banks, building societies and insurance companies and affects those who enter into regulated mortgage contracts, i.e. first legal mortgages of land intended for residential occupation.

*The 2006 Act*

Sections 19–22 import a new approach which allows the court to determine whether the relationship between lender and borrower is unfair to the borrower because of the terms of the credit agreement, the way in which the agreement is operated by the lender or because of anything done or not done by the lender either prior to or subsequent to the agreement. In reaching its decision the court may take into account any matters that it considers relevant. The 2006 Act does not, however, apply to the majority of mortgages because it expressly excludes those within the **Financial Services and Markets Act 2000**. Its scope in the mortgage market will be limited to the second (i.e. non-acquisition) mortgage market.

## RIGHTS AND REMEDIES OF THE MORTGAGE LENDER

Where a mortgagor defaults under the terms of the mortgage the mortgagee is given various rights and remedies. These include the right to take possession and the remedies of sale, foreclosure, suing on the personal covenant to repay and the appointment of a receiver. These remedies are in general cumulative; for example, if sale realises less than the mortgage debt then the mortgagee may sue on the personal covenant: *Bristol & West Plc v Bartlett* (2003).

Figure 13

Mortgagee's Remedies

Sue on Personal Covenant to Repay
— Capital (12 Years)
— Interest (6 Years)

Foreclosure
— Court Order
— Can be Reopened

Sale
— Power Arisen
— Power Exercisable

Receiver
— Power Arisen
— Power Exercisable

### Possession

The mortgagee's right to take possession arises automatically at common law and is exercisable even if the mortgagor is not in default: *Four Maids Ltd v Dudley Marshall Properties Ltd* (1957). There Harman J. famously remarked that a mortgagee can take possession, "before the ink is dry on the mortgage". In practice, however, possession will be sought only if the mortgagor is in breach of the mortgage agreement. This is because the modern lender is interested in money and not in turning people out of their homes. In addition, a mortgagee who takes possession is under certain duties, for example, to keep the property in reasonable repair and to account strictly for any rents and profits received. If the mortgagee leases the property, the lender must get the best possible rent: *White v City of London Brewery* (1889).

### Court order

Usually, a court order for possession will be necessary in order to shield the lender from criminal and civil liability under s.6 of the Criminal Law Act 1977. Such an order is not necessary, however, if the premises are unoccupied or when the borrower has left willingly (*Ropaigealach v Barclays Bank Plc* (1999)). On the lender's application for possession of a dwelling house, the court has a statutory discretion to adjourn the proceedings or to grant a stay of execution of any order: s.36 of the Administration of Justice Act 1970 (as amended by s.8 of the AJA 1973).

### Section 36

This statutory discretion is available only if it seems likely that, within a reasonable time, the mortgagor will be able to pay any sums due or be able to remedy any other breach of the mortgage. In *Cheltenham & Gloucester Building Society v Norgan* (1996), there were 13 years remaining on the mortgage, the house was worth £225,000 and the amount owed was £97,000. The lender's position was secure and the court could afford to be generous. The Court of Appeal set out much needed guidance as to how the court's discretion should be exercised:

- it established the working rule that a reasonable time will be the remaining years of the mortgage;
- the borrower is expected to produce a detailed budget to convince the court that it is likely that the arrears will be paid off as well as meeting future payments as they fall due;
- if the new arrangement is broken, the courts are unlikely to give the borrower a second chance;
- the Norgan approach operates only when there is the ability to discharge the arrears on an installment basis and when there is no negative equity. A negative equity arises when the property is worth less than the debt owed. In *Realkredit Danmark v Brookfield House* (2000), however, this was not the case and the court ordered immediate possession. There more than £2 million was owed, but the property was worth only £1.5 million. The lender's interests were in real jeopardy.

## Sale

A statutory power of sale is given by the **Law of Property Act 1925**. This was necessary because at common law there is no power of sale. The 1925 Act draws a distinction between when that power arises and when it becomes exercisable. Where the power of sale has arisen (s.101), the mortgagee can give a good title to a purchaser free from the equity of redemption even if the power has been irregularly exercised: s.104. Consequently, a purchaser need only verify that the power of sale has arisen and this can usually be done by inspection of the mortgage deed. If the power has not arisen, however, the purchaser will merely get an assignment of the benefit of the existing mortgage.

### Power arising

The power arises under s.101 subject to three conditions:

- the power is not excluded in the mortgage deed. For obvious reasons, such exclusion would be rare except where the lender wishes to replace it with a wider private power of sale;
- the mortgage is made by deed. This includes all legal mortgages, but excludes most equitable mortgages as they will usually be created informally; and
- the legal redemption date has passed, i.e. the date specified in the mortgage agreement as the redemption date. This is normally six months after the mortgage is created.

### Becoming exercisable

The power is exercisable under s.103 where either:

- notice requiring payment of the entire mortgage money has been served by the lender and this has not been complied with by the borrower within three months. This refers to capital payments;
- some interest under the mortgage is two months in arrears and unpaid; or,
- there is a breach of some other mortgage covenant (e.g. to insure or to keep in repair).

### Proceeds of sale

The effect of a valid sale is to vest the whole estate of the mortgagor in the purchaser subject to any superior (or prior) mortgages. Although the selling mortgagee will receive the purchase money, s.105 provides that after sale the proceeds are to be held on trust and to be used to pay in declining order:

(i)     any superior mortgages;
(ii)    the expenses of the sale;
(iii)   the principal, interest and costs of the selling lender's mortgage;
(iv)    any inferior mortgages; and
(v)     as regards the residue (if any), the mortgagor.

### Lender not a trustee of power

The lender is not a trustee of the power of sale: *Nash v Eads* (1880). For example, there is no duty to sell as quickly as possible: *China & South Seas Bank v Tan* (1990). A mortgagee, moreover, does not usually need a court order to execute sale. The discretion to sell the mortgaged property in order to achieve repayment of the debt owed is largely unfettered. For example, the lender need not delay sale until planning permission is obtained or leases granted in order to obtain a better price: *Silven Properties v Royal Bank of Scotland* (2003). In *AIB Finance Ltd v Alsop* (1998), a post office had been closed by the borrower and the court held that there was no duty on the lender to sell the business as a going concern.

### Good faith

The lender must act in good faith which entails that it cannot sell the property to itself (*Tse Kwong Lam v Wong Chit Sen* (1983)) or sell it quickly at a knock down price (*Palk v Mortgages Services Funding* (1993)). If the sale is achieved at an undervalue, the court will interfere only when there is fraud, negligence or bad faith on the part of the lender: *Cuckmere Brick Co Ltd v Mutual Finance* (1971). In addition, a borrower can specifically agree to a sale at less than market price and, if this occurs, he will be estopped from asserting a claim against the lender: *Mercantile Credit Co v Clarke* (1997).

### Price to be obtained

The lender's obligation is to obtain the best price reasonably obtainable for the property in the condition it is in when sold: *Cuckmere Brick Co Ltd v Mutual Finance* (1971). This means the same as a "proper price" and "the true market value of the mortgaged property": *Michael v Miller* (2004). There Jonathan Parker L.J. explained:

> "Subject to any restrictions in the mortgage deed, it is for the mortgagee to decide whether the sale should be by public auction or private treaty,

just as it is for him to decide how the sale should be advertised and how long the property should be left on the market."

The mortgagee must, however, make an informed judgment in exercising the power of sale and this will involve the taking of advice (including valuation advice) from a duly qualified agent: *Tse Kwong Lam v Wong Chit Sen* (1983). In calculating the market value the court will adopt a "bracket concept", i.e. there will be no undervalue if the valuation falls within an acceptable margin of error. In *Michael v Miller* (2004), for example, the bracket of acceptable valuation spanned £1.6 million to £1.9 million.

## Judicial Sale
In addition to the statutory power given specifically to legal mortgagees, the court is afforded a general power to order sale at the instance of any "person interested": s.91 of the **LPA**. This may, for example, be as an alternative to foreclosure (see below): *Twentieth Century Banking v Wilkinson* (1977). It can also be employed by an equitable mortgagee or, indeed, by the borrower himself when the mortgagee will not agree to a private sale (e.g. there is a negative equity): *Cheltenham & Gloucester Building Society v Krausz* (1996). In *Palk v Mortgage Services Funding* (1993), the lender wished to lease the mortgaged property until the market improved whereas the borrower wanted an outright sale. Even though it would produce a negative equity, the borrower obtained a court order for sale under s.91.

## Foreclosure
Foreclosure is the most draconian weapon in the armoury of the lender. As will become understandable, the court is reluctant to order foreclosure and will almost inevitably grant sale instead: *Palk v Mortgage Services Funding* (1993). Foreclosure amounts to a total confiscation of the borrower's interest in the property. In a foreclosure action the court declares that the mortgagor's equitable right to redeem is extinguished and the mortgagee becomes owner at law and in equity. The remedy disregards the fact that the property might be worth more than the debt outstanding and discounts any repayments made over previous years.

### Illustration

X buys a house in 2000 for £100,000 with the assistance of a £80,000 mortgage. In 2010, the house is worth £170,000 and the mortgage is now £70,000. In that year X is made redundant and can no longer afford the monthly mortgage repayments. At the time of purchase, X enjoyed a £20,000 equity in the property and this had, by 2010, risen to £100,000. If the lender sells the property, X is entitled to the balance remaining after discharge of the mortgage debt and expenses. If the lender can foreclose, X gets nothing. The mortgage obtains a windfall of £100,000.

### Limitations

There are three limitations upon the remedy of foreclosure:

* the legal date for redemption must have passed (see above);
* there must be a court order. The mortgagee must bring an action in the High Court and all parties interested must be made parties to the action (e.g. the borrower, any other mortgagees and any tenant of the mortgagor). The court will issue a foreclosure order nisi, which will require the mortgagor to repay what is due on or before a specified date (generally six months hence). In default the order is made absolute. This does not mean that it is final because foreclosure can be reopened by the court at any time while the lender holds the property and the borrower's equity of redemption thereby revived: *Campbell v Holyland* (1877); and
* in proceedings any "person interested", namely the mortgagor or subsequent mortgagee, may apply for judicial sale rather than foreclosure: s.91 of the **LPA**. This alternative order will then usually be granted.

## Appointment of a Receiver

This is the appointment of a person or company with management powers who may collect rents and profits arising from the mortgaged land. This is relevant to non-residential mortgages only as there has to be some income to receive. The statutory power to appoint is given by s.101 of the **LPA** and arises in the same way as the power of sale. This remedy is most commonly used where the mortgagor has leased the property and rents and profits can thereby be intercepted. The mortgage agreement will usually designate the receiver as the agent of the mortgagor, but this is no true agency. The mortgagor does not appoint the receiver, cannot give him instructions and cannot sack him. Indeed, there exists no contractual relationship between them and the duties of the receiver are owed in equity to both the borrower and the lender: *Silven Properties Ltd v Royal Bank of Scotland* (2003). The receiver's primary function is to exercise his management powers to try and ensure that the debt is repaid, i.e. for the benefit of the lender.

### Use of income

The receiver must apply any income received in the following order:

(i) payment of rent, rates and taxes;
(ii) payment of interest on any incumbrances having priority to the mortgage;

(iii)   the receiver's commission, premiums and cost of repairs;

(iv)   interest on the mortgage;

(v)   if the mortgagee so directs in writing, payment towards the discharge of the principal sum; and

(vi)   any surplus to the person next entitled (e.g. inferior mortgagees or the mortgagor).

### Receiver's duty

The extent of a receiver's duty to the mortgagor was reviewed by the Court of Appeal in *Medforth v Blake* (1999). The court stated that, where a receiver manages property, his duty to the mortgagor and anyone else interested in the equity of redemption was not necessarily confined to a duty of good faith. Rather, in exercising a power of management the receiver owes a duty to manage the property with due diligence subject to a primary duty of attempting to create a situation where the interest on the secured debt could be paid and the debt itself repaid. Due diligence does not necessarily oblige the receiver to continue in business at the mortgaged property nor, as a pre-requisite to sale, to obtain planning permission or to grant leases.

## Right to Sue on the Personal Covenant to Repay

In all mortgage deeds, there is a covenant to repay interest and capital. As with any contractual debt, the mortgagee can sue the borrower for the amount outstanding. Section 8 of the Limitation Act 1980 provides that the right to sue for the capital sum will be statute-barred after 12 years if the mortgage is created by deed (this is called a "specialty" debt). If the mortgage is not created by deed, a similar limitation period applies by virtue of s.24(1). As to suing for interest, the limitation period is six years (s.20(5)). The limitation periods begin to run from the date of the borrower's default: *Wilkinson v West Bromwich Building Society* (2004).

## Miscellaneous Rights

- The right to lease and accept surrenders: ss.99 and 100 of the **LPA**.
- The right to fixtures attached to the mortgage property (i.e. they become part of the security for the loan).
- In unregistered land, the right to possession of the title deeds (ss.85 and 86 of the **LPA**) and an obligation to redeliver them on redemption.
- The right to insure the mortgaged property: ss.101 and 108 of the **LPA**.

## Tacking and Consolidation
### Tacking

The right to tack further advances entails that, In certain circumstances, a mortgagee may demand repayment of several loans in priority to lenders who made intervening loans. It is an amalgamation of one mortgage with another by the same lender of a higher priority. This is a method of leap-frogging the basic rules on priority of mortgages.

### Consolidation

The right of consolidation which applies where there are mortgages of more than one property held by the same lender. It is the right of a lender in whom two or more mortgages are vested to refuse to allow redemption of one without redemption of the others. The right will not exist unless the following conditions can be satisfied:

- the right to consolidate must expressly be given in one of the mortgage deeds: s.93(1) of the **LPA**;
- the legal redemption dates on both mortgages must have passed;
- both mortgages must have been made by the same mortgagor; and
- at some stage both mortgages must have been vested in one person and at the same time both equities of redemption were vested in another. This is termed the simultaneous union of mortgages and equities.

## Equitable Mortgagees
An equitable mortgagee has many of the rights and powers of a legal mortgagee, but there are some major differences.

### Sale

Only if the mortgage is made by deed, does the equitable mortgagee enjoy the right to sell under s.101–103 of the **LPA**. Otherwise, the court may order a sale by virtue of its s.91 power.

### Foreclosure

Equitable mortgagees may go for foreclosure because they do not generally have a power of sale in the knowledge that, instead, the court will order sale under s.91.

### Possession

The equitable mortgagee has no right at law to possession because he holds no legal estate: *Ashley Guarantee Plc v Zacaria* (1993). If, however, sale is ordered by the court, the court will also order that vacant possession be given.

### Appointment of a receiver

A statutory power under the **LPA** exists if the mortgage was made by deed. If no deed exists, the court also has an inherent power to make an appointment.

### Suing on the personal covenant

The mortgagor can be sued personally for the recovery of the debt. Whether or not the mortgage is made by deed, there is a 12 year limitation period for capital (six years for interest) within which the lender must commence proceedings for recovery of the debt.

| Revision Checklist | O |
|---|---|

You should now know and understand:

- how mortgages are created;

- the right of the borrower to redeem and how that right is protected;

- the mortgagee's right to possession and the court's s.36 discretion;

- the mortgagee's remedies;

- the different rules which apply to equitable mortgages.

## QUESTION AND ANSWER

### Question

In 2006, Hugh borrowed £50,000 from Jack secured by a first legal mortgage of Hugh's registered freehold property, the White House. In October 2008 Hugh borrowed a further £13,000 from Pam, secured by a second legal mortgage on the White House. Hugh has now fallen into arrears with his payments of interest due under the second mortgage.

a) Explain in what circumstances Pam could sell the White House to secure repayment of her loan and how any such sale would affect Jack's position.

b) If in the exercise of any power of sale she may have Pam sells the White House at less than its open market value, would Hugh have any remedy against Pam or a purchaser from Pam?

c) How must Pam apply the proceeds of any such sale of the White House and what special precautions must she take in doing so?

## Advice and the Answer

a) A power of sale arises in accordance with **LPA 1925** s.101, if the mortgage has been made by deed, the legal date for redemption has passed and the power has not been excluded in the mortgage deed. If the mortgage is to be paid by instalments, this arises as soon as any instalment is in arrears. The power of sale is exercisable under the terms of **LPA** s.103, when one of three conditions is satisfied, namely that some interest under the mortgage is at least two months in arrears; that there has been three months' default in repayment of the loan after notice requiring it has been served on the mortgagor; or that there has been a breach of some covenant in the mortgage deed (other than for repayment of mortgage money or interest). It should, however, be noted that these statutory powers may be varied or extended by the mortgage deed. The question does not indicate the extent of the arrears in the payment of interest under Pam's mortgage, but if that interest is at least two months in arrears the power of sale has become exercisable. The mortgage is legal and s.101 consequently appears to have been complied with (the legal redemption date often being six months after the creation of the mortgage).

As to Jack's position as a prior mortgagee, any sale by Pam is subject to his mortgage: **LPA** s.104(1) and on a sale he is entitled to have first claim to the proceeds of sale

b) Although Pam is not a trustee for the borrower, she must act in good faith. There is no obligation on her to sell by auction or to advertise the property. As a general rule sale at a low price will not be interfered with in the absence of fraud or negligence. If a sale takes place at less than the open market value this raises an inference of lack of good faith and damages may be awarded. In *Cuckmere Brick Co Ltd v Mutual Finance Ltd*, where damages were awarded to compensate for a sale of a plot of land where full particulars had not been given, it was stated by Salmon L.J. that "a mortgagee in exercising his power of sale owes a duty to take reasonable precautions to obtain the true market value of the mortgaged property on the date on which he decides to sell". Pam cannot sell the property to herself either directly or through an agent as this would not be a *bona fide* sale: *Tse Kwong Lam v Wong Chit Sen*.

If Hugh agrees with Pam that the property can be sold at less than the market price, Hugh will be estopped from relying on any duty of care that may exist provided there was no evidence of undue or unconscionable action on Pam's part: *Mercantile Credit Co v Clarke*. If Pam fails to observe any required duty in exercising the sale and sells at an artificially low price, then damages may be payable to Hugh. In *Tomlin v Lace*, where a mortgagee had misdescribed the property he had to make an allowance to the purchaser from the price and was held liable to the mortgagor for the difference.

Once the power of sale has arisen (s.101) the mortgagee can give a good title to the purchaser free from the equity of redemption, even if the power of sale has not become exercisable: s.104. If the purchaser is aware of any facts showing that the power of sale has not become exercisable or that there is any impropriety in the sale, he will not get a good title. Consequently, any purchaser from Pam would obtain a good title provided he was not aware that the sale was abnormally low or that there was any fraud, bad faith or impropriety involved.

c) Pam must pay off the prior mortgage of Jack and apply the remainder of the proceeds of sale in accordance with s.105 which makes Pam a trustee of those proceeds to be applied in the following order:

- to pay the expenses of the sale;
- to pay the principal sum, interest and costs of the selling mortgagee's loan;
- to pay the residue to the next incumbrancer, but if none then what remains is to be paid to the mortgagor.

Pam must make sure that in paying over the residue it is to the person best entitled. She should check in the relevant register to determine whether any later mortgages have been registered, and if so this amounts to notice to her. If she pays the residue to Hugh without making this inquiry and it transpires that subsequent mortgagees exist there will be liability.

# Licences

## 13

## INTRODUCTION

A licence is mere permission to be on land, i.e. it prevents what would otherwise be an unlawful trespass: *Thomas v Sorrell* (1673). Licences, moreover, do not give the licensee a property interest: *Ashburn Anstalt v Arnold* (1989). Accordingly, a licence is not transferable and, being only a personal right, will not be enforceable against third parties: *Clore v Theatrical Properties* (1936).

## TYPES OF LICENCE

**Figure 14**

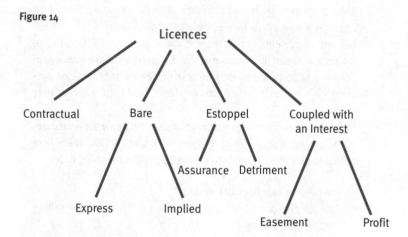

### The Bare Licence

Where the licensee provides no consideration it is called a bare or gratuitous licence. A bare licence can be created expressly, e.g. where you invite someone into your home for dinner or to stay overnight. It can also arise through implication, e.g. a gate and pathway leading to the front door of a house offers an implied licence to use that gate and path for the lawful purposes of, say, delivering leaflets and attracting the attention of the occupier: *Robson v Hallett* (1967). A bare licence is revocable, by words or actions, at any time on giving reasonable notice: *Re Hampstead Garden Suburb Institute* (1995). Of course, what is reasonable depends upon the circumstances and, in particular, the nature of the permission to be revoked. If the licensee refuses to leave or exceeds the ambit of what was permitted, he becomes a trespasser and can be removed by reasonable force: *Tomlinson v Congleton BC* (2004).

## The Contractual Licence
This is a licence that is supported by consideration, i.e. it arises under the terms of a contract. Such a licence will emerge when you pay for admission to a cinema, concert venue or football ground. For example, when you enter a bar you are a bare licensee. At that stage, you can be asked to leave immediately (in the circumstances that would be reasonable notice) and there is nothing you can do. Once you order a drink, however, you become a contractual licensee. A contractual licence can be revoked in accordance with its terms (e.g. on the expiry of time) or, if no mention is made of termination, on reasonable notice: *Winter Garden Theatre (London) Ltd v Millenium Productions Ltd* (1948). Hence, the bar should allow you sufficient time to consume your beverage before asking you to leave. If not, you can (in theory) bring an action for breach of contract and will have a claim for compensation. In *Wood v Leadbitter* (1845) for example, damages were awarded to an individual who was ejected from a Doncaster race meeting. On occasion, however, the court may be willing to grant equitable remedies.

### Equitable remedies

In *Winter Garden Theatre (London) Ltd v Millenium Productions Ltd* (1948), it was acknowledged by the House of Lords that an injunction might be used to preserve the sanctity of bargain underlying a contractual licence when it was an express or implied term that it could not be revoked. This approach cannot, however, protect a bare licensee since equity will not assist a volunteer. In *Verrall v Great Yarmouth BC* (1980), specific performance of a contract for the hire of a hall by the National Front was granted and the purported revocation by the local Conservative council, in breach of contract, was resisted. On the facts, damages were thought to be inadequate because the National Front would not have been able to find anywhere else to hold its two day conference. If sufficient notice had been give to the licensee, damages would presumably have been awarded instead. It seems that Verrall emphasises the consequences of the breach rather than the nature of the contractual licence itself. It is to be appreciated that, had the Council sold on the premises, the National Front would not have been able to enforce the contract against the third party purchaser (*King v David Allen & Sons* (1916)).

## Licence Coupled with an Interest
This type of arrangement arises where a licence is implied as ancillary to the grant of a property right, e.g. an easement or a profit a prendre. Albeit uncommon in

modern times, the right to hunt animals, fish, or cut timber may all imply a permission to enter on the land. As the property right is irrevocable, so must be the
attendant licence. Hence, albeit indirectly, it has the potential to bind a purchaser
as the shadow of the property right: *Wood v Leadbitter* (1845).

## The Estoppel Licence

At the core of an estoppel is the notion that some form of assurance (whether
by words or conduct) has been made and detrimentally relied upon by the other
party: *Willmott v Barber* (1880). The assurance must be clear and the expectation of the other party must be that it is binding: *Cobbe v Yeoman's Row
Management Ltd* (2008). Detrimental reliance or change of position can include
monetary expenditure, the exertion of labour or bringing about a change of
conduct or circumstances. The reliance must be reasonable and must be known
(or should have been known) to the person making the assurance. In such situations, it would be unjust and unconscionable for the person making the
assurance to rely upon his strict legal rights. Instead, that person is said to be
"estopped" from resiling from that assurance. Hence, if an owner of land permits, promises or acquiesces in the use of land by another he may be estopped
from denying that person's right to use the land. As an estoppel is a property
right it can bind third parties and, in doing so, will protect the licence which it
encases: *Ives v High* (1967).

### *Illustrative cases*

- In *Dodsworth v Dodsworth* (1973), expenditure by a couple on improvements to a bungalow, after being encouraged and induced by an assurance that they could live there as their home for as long as they wished,
  created an estoppel allowing occupation until the expenditure had been
  reimbursed;
- in *Pascoe v Turner* (1979), a woman had lived with her lover in his house.
  He had assured her that on his death the house and everything in it would
  be hers. On the strength of this she expended money on repairs and
  improvements. An estoppel was created and, following his death, the
  court ordered that the property be conveyed to her;
- in *Inwards v Baker* (1965), a father encouraged his son to build a bungalow
  on his (the father's) land. The court held that the son had a right to occupy
  the land for as long as he wished;
- in *Crabb v Arun DC* (1976), an assurance was given that the claimant
  would be allowed a right of access across the defendant's land. In reliance on this statement, the claimant sold other land that would have
  provided an alternative access. The defendant was estopped from denying the right of access.

*Satisfying the estoppel*

Once an estoppel has arisen, it is up to the court how it is to be satisfied. In many cases, this may simply mean giving effect to the assurance. The court is, however, unable to go beyond what was informally assured: *Orgee v Orgee* (1997). In each case, the court will order what it believes to be appropriate satisfaction having regard to the assurance and the reliance placed upon it. As illustrative in *Jennings v Rice* (2003), the court will award the minimum equity so as to do justice. For example:

- by enforcing the terms of an informal agreement: *JT Developments Ltd v Quinn* (1992);
- by giving a right to occupy; *Greasley v Cooke* (1980);
- by perfecting an oral gift and ordering the transfer of title to the property: *Voyce v Voyce* (1991);
- by declaring one of two joint tenants to be the sole beneficial owner: *Lim Teng Huan v Ang Swee Chuan* (1992) or ordering the transfer of the legal estate to the claimant *Dillwynn Llewelyn* (1862);
- by ordering a refund of the cost of any expenditure plus interest: *Burrows v Sharp* (1991);
- by awarding the claimant a monetary interest in a house: *Jennings v Rice* (2003)

## Revision Checklist

You should now know and understand:

- **what is a licence;**

- **the differences between the various types of licence;**

- **the types of remedies available for breach of licence agreement.**

# QUESTION AND ANSWER

## Question

a) Last year, a controversial political party called the National Affront booked a hall from Billy in which to hold their annual conference. Recently, its leader appeared on a television program and made certain outrageous comments concerning immigration. Billy is deeply offended by these remarks and writes to the National Affront cancelling its booking. The National Affront has found it impossible to find alternative accommodation and fear that it will no longer be able to hold the conference.

b) This year, Billy has allowed his disabled aunt, Molly, to live in one of his houses. He assures her that she will be able to live there as long as she wants and, in return, she agrees to install a new central heating system and double glazing. She also pays for expensive conversion works to the property in order to cater for her specialist needs. Billy now wishes to sell the house with vacant possession.

Advise the National Affront and Molly.

## Advice and the Answer

a) The National Affront has entered into a contractual licence with Billy. At common law, the contractual licence is revocable at any time. If it is not terminated in accordance with its terms, however, the revocation will amount to a breach of contract and entitled the licensee to damages for any loss rising: *Wood v Leadbitter*. This form of redress is not probably what the National Affront would wish for as it cannot find alternative premises. The National Affront would, in all likelihood, prefer that it could still hold its conference in Billy's hall. This would require the intervention of Equity and this might take the form of the grant of an injunction or the specific performance of the contract. As regards the former, in *Winter Garden Theatre (London) Ltd v Millenium Productions Ltd* the court was able to imply a contractual term which restrained the premature revocation of the contractual licence. This implied obligation can then be enforced by an injunction prohibiting the wrongful breach of contract. As the licence was designed to cater for a specific event, such a term could be implied in favour of the National Affront. In relation to specific performance, the decision in *Verrall v Great Yarmouth BC* assumes importance. There the booking of a hall for a political rally was specifically enforced against the unwilling local authority.

b) Molly is in occupation Billy's house. There is no valid contract between the pair and there is no tenancy. She has a mere licence to occupy for as long as she wishes. In order to resist any possible sale by Billy, she will have to assert an estoppel which can be used to prevent sale or, as demonstrated in *Jennings v Rice*, ensure that her rights will bind any future purchaser. Molly will have to show that

Billy made an assurance (which he did) and that she changed her position substantially on the strength of that assurance (which she did). Hence, she can establish an estoppel to protect her licence as occurred in *Dodsworth v Dodsworth* and *Inwards v Baker*. As to how the estoppel will be satisfied, the court has the discretion to award "minimum equity" in the light of all the factors (e.g. the money that she has spent on the property and the rent free accommodation promised and already enjoyed). She cannot obtain more than was represented: *Orgee v Orgee*. In Molly's case, this may well entail that, due to the expenses incurred and her age, she will be entitled to live in the property for as long as she wants. This is as occurred in *Inwards v Baker* and *Greasley v Cooke*.

# Freehold Covenants

## 14

## INTRODUCTION

A covenant is a formal promise contained in a deed whereby one party undertakes to another party that he will or will not carry out some specific activity on his land. This chapter is concerned with the situation where one fee simple owner (freeholder) covenants in favour of another either positively (e.g. to construct or maintain a road) or negatively (e.g. not to build shops or conduct a certain business on his land). Hence, a freehold covenant imposes controls over land use. Negative freehold covenants offer an equitable interest in the burdened land. Although the covenants will be binding between the contracting parties, the major issue concerns the circumstances in which they will be enforceable by and against future purchasers of the relevant properties. All turns upon the capacity in law or in equity for the benefit and the burden of the covenant to run with the land. For example, A sells part of Whiteacre to B. A covenants in the conveyance that he will not build on the part retained. A (the "covenantor") later sells the retained land to C. B (the "covenantee") then sells his land to D. The central concern for D is whether he can enforce the covenant against C.

## ORIGINAL PARTIES

### Exceptions to Privity of Contract

As between the original parties to the covenant there is privity of contract and the original covenantee can enforce the express covenant against the original covenantor. At common law only parties to a deed could sue upon it, but this rule is now subject to statutory qualifications.

### *Section 136 of the Law of Property Act 1925*

This permits the benefit of a covenant to be expressly assigned in writing to some other person. The assignee then stands in the shoes of the assignor and can enforce the covenant in his own right. This does not apply to the burden of a covenant.

### Section 56(1) of the LPA

This allows enforcement by persons other than a named party to the deed, provided such persons are identifiable at the time of the deed: *Re Ecclesiastical Commissioners for England's Conveyance* (1936). In order to be within the ambit of s.56, a person must show that the covenant was intended to benefit him, even though he was not a party to the deed: *Beswick v Beswick* (1968). Consequently a reference to successors in title is not enough for the purposes of s.56 as they are not ascertainable at the time the covenant is created: *Kelsey v Dodd* (1881). Once s.56 gives the benefit to an individual (who is then treated as having been an original covenantee), the benefit can then pass to his successors. This does not apply to the burden of a covenant.

### Section 1 of the Contracts (Rights of Third Parties) Act 1999

This also permits someone other than the direct covenantee to enforce the covenant. The 1999 Act applies where the covenant identifies the third party either by name or as a member of a class (e.g. successors in title). The third party need not be in existence when the covenant is entered. This does not apply to the burden of a covenant.

## THE RUNNING OF COVENANTS

### Meaning

When a covenant is enforceable by and against successors in title of the original covenantor and covenantee, it is often said to "run with the land". This means that the benefit and burden of the covenant are capable of being transmitted when the respective properties are sold off. In deciding whether a covenant runs with the land there are two sets of principles: the common law rules and the equitable rules. Each must be examined separately. The common law rules should be applied first, as it is only if they are inapplicable that the equitable rules need be employed. The benefit of both positive and negative covenants can pass at common law, but the equitable rules apply only to negative (i.e. restrictive covenants): *Gafford v Graham* (1998).

Figure 15

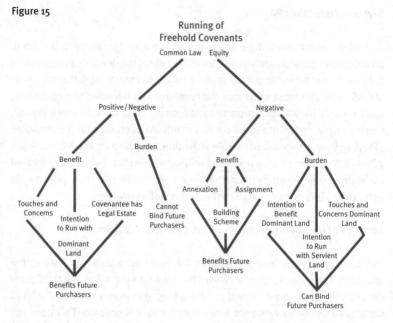

Running of
Freehold Covenants

## Common Law Rules
### Burden

The burden of a covenant (regardless of whether it is positive or negative in nature) cannot run with the land: *Austerberry v Oldham Corp* (1885). Consequently, only a person who is an actual party to the covenant can be sued at common law. Hence, if the original covenantor sells on the land the covenant cannot be enforced against the new purchaser. The statutory relaxation of the privity of contract rules (e.g. under the **Contracts (Rights of Third Parties) Act 1999**) does not apply to the burden of a covenant.

### Benefit

As shown the benefit of a positive or negative freehold covenant may be assigned in writing to a third party. It can also pass at common law subject to the conditions set out in *P&A Swift Investments v Combined English Stores Group Plc* (1989).

### Conditions

- The covenant must touch and concern (i.e. benefit) the land of the covenantee, i.e. the covenant must not be merely personal in nature. In *Smith & Snipes Hall Farm Ltd v River Douglas Catchment Board* (1949), it was made clear that this requirement must either affect the land as regards mode of occupation or affect directly the value of the land.

- The covenantee must, at the time of the covenant, have a legal estate in land to be benefited. This is because equitable interests in land were not historically recognised by the common law courts. An assignee need not, however, have the same legal estate as the covenantee. In the *Smith & Snipes* case, a tenant acquired the benefit of a covenant made with a predecessor in title who was a freeholder. It is not required that the covenantor have any estate in land.
- The covenant must have been intended to run with the land owned by the original covenantee. No contrary intention should be expressed in the conveyance to the effect that the covenant was not intended to run with the land: *Rogers v Hosegood* (1900). In the absence of such contrary indication, s.78 of the **LPA** deems the covenant to have been made on behalf of successors in title.

## Equitable Rules and Negative Covenants
### Burden

The burden of a negative covenant can run with the land in equity. The burden of a positive covenant cannot: *Rhone v Stephens* (1994). The decision in *Tulk v Moxhay* (1848) allegedly fathered what is now known as the law of restrictive covenants. The burden can run on the satisfaction of certain conditions.

### The covenant must be negative/restrictive in nature

For these purposes it is the substance and not the form or outward appearance of the covenant that is crucial. In *Tulk v Moxhay*, the covenant was to keep and maintain a garden in Leicester Square in an open state and uncovered by buildings. Although expressed in a positive voice (i.e. to do something), it was in reality a covenant not to do something (i.e. not to build) and, therefore, a negative covenant. As a rule of thumb, if the covenant requires the expenditure of money in its performance (e.g. to maintain a roof) then it will be positive: *Haywood v Brunswick Permanent Benefit Building Society* (1888). A covenant which has both positive and negative elements can be severed so that the negative element will be binding on the land: *Shepherd Homes Ltd v Sandham (No. 2)* (1971).

### The covenant must benefit the covenantee's dominant land

Subject to statutory modification, for the burden of a restrictive covenant to run there must be both a dominant and a servient tenement. If a covenantee does not own or retain adjacent land capable of benefiting from the restriction, the covenant is merely personal in nature and, as such, enforceable only between the original parties: *Formby v Barker* (1903). This is a question of fact and physical proximity is a crucial factor in showing that the dominant land is benefited. In *Kelly v Barrett* (1924), it was stated that "covenants binding land in Hampstead will be too remote to benefit land in Clapham". The covenant itself must either affect the land as regards mode of occupation, or it must be such as to directly, and not merely from collateral circumstances, affect the value of the land: *Rogers v Hosegood* (1900). It has to be something more than personal convenience and advantage. For example, in *Newton Abbot Co-op v Williamson & Treadgold Ltd* (1952) a covenant designed to prevent trade competition was held to touch and concern as it benefited a trade carried out on the dominant land. As to what constitutes the dominant tenement, it was held in *Re Ballard's Conveyance* (1937) that the dominant tenement must be clearly identified. There the dominant tenement was the whole of an estate consisting of 1,700 acres and the covenant was held to be ineffective because it could not directly benefit the whole of that estate. If, however, a covenant is annexed expressly or impliedly to the "whole and each and every part" of the dominant land, it is enforceable by the successors in title to any part which actually benefits from it: *Robins v Berkeley Homes* (1996).

### The burden must be intended to run with the covenantor's servient land

Although this might be expressed or inferred from the wording of the covenant itself, s.79 of the **LPA** provides that, in the absence of a contrary intention expressed in the conveyance, a covenant is deemed to run with the land. The presumption is that the covenant was made "by the covenantor on behalf of himself his successors in title and the persons deriving title under him or them".

### Operation of section 79

- Lord Upjohn in *Tophams Ltd v Earl of Sefton* (1967) explained that s.79, "does no more than render it unnecessary in the description of the parties to the conveyance to add after the respondent's name: his executors, administrators and assigns";
- in *Morrells of Oxford Ltd v Oxford United FC Ltd* (2001), the covenant was given by the City Council to the predecessor in title of Morrells of Oxford. The covenant prevented the City Council permitting any land within a half mile radius of the dominant tenement being used as a brewery, club or licensed premises. Oxford United bought land from the City Council within this radius and, as part of its stadium development, wanted to open a hotel and sell alcohol from various outlets. It was clear that, unless s.79 operated, the covenant would be merely personal as it made no mention of successors in title. Morrells attempted to rely upon s.79, but the Court

of Appeal held that a contrary intention existed which prevented such reliance. The obstacle was that the conveyance had adopted an inconsistency of style between the drafting of landlord's covenants and tenant's covenants. The tenant's covenants were expressly made to bind future tenants whereas, as noted, the landlord's covenants were not. This contrast demonstrated an intention to exclude s.79 and, therefore, the covenant could not bind Oxford United.

### Binding a purchaser

The burden will bind a purchaser of the servient land only when the covenant is registered. In unregistered land, this is done by the entry of a D(ii) land charge as regards covenants created after 1925. In relation to pre-1926 covenants, they are still subject to the doctrine of notice which means that, because freehold covenants are necessarily equitable interests, they bind everyone except a bona fide purchaser of the legal estate for value without notice. As regards registered land, the **Land Registration Act 2002** requires a restrictive covenant to be protected by the entry of a notice on the Charges Register of the servient land.

## Benefit

The benefit of a negative covenant can run in equity. It is, perhaps, a subject of initial confusion that there are two sets of rules (albeit similar) relating to the benefit of covenants: the common law rules (see above) and the equitable rules (now to be considered). The real distinction is that, with negative covenants, the remedy sought by the dominant owner will be an injunction preventing breach by the servient owner. As this is an equitable remedy, it is necessary to show that the conditions of equity as to benefit are satisfied. In addition, the equitable rules must always operate when the servient tenement has been sold on. The straightforward rule is, therefore, that the burden of the covenant is unenforceable in equity unless the benefit of the covenant has also run in equity: *J Sainsbury Ltd v Enfield LBC* (1989). In the eyes of equity, the benefit can pass in one of three ways: annexation, assignment and under a building scheme.

### Express annexation

This is the linking of the covenant to the benefited land and is achieved by express words in the covenant itself. Once the benefit is annexed it runs with the land automatically even if the successor to the land does not know it exists when he takes the conveyance. In *Rogers v Hosegood* (1900), express annexation occurred due to the use of the words, "his successors and assigns and others claiming under him or them to all or any of his land adjoining . . . the said premises". It is, however, crucial that the benefited land be referred to because, without this identification, there can be no annexation. This means that a covenant merely with the "vendors, their heirs, executors, administrators and assigns" is insufficient for there is no reference to any land. A successor to a part of land must show that the benefit is annexed to that part: *Formby v Barker* (1903). Accordingly, it is better practice to annex the covenant to the whole and to each and every part of the dominant tenement: *Zetland v Driver* (1939).

### Statutory annexation

This is catered for by s.78 of the **LPA** and this facility goes some way to overcome the problems of annexation by express words in the conveyance. Section 78 states that:

> "a covenant relating to any land of the covenantee shall be deemed to be made with the covenantee, and his successors in title and the persons deriving title under him or them, and shall have effect as if such successors and other persons were expressed".

The provision dispenses with the need for express words. In *Federated Homes Ltd v Mill Lodge Properties Ltd* (1980), it was held that the purpose of s.78 was to effect annexation to the land as a whole and to each and every part. In *Roake v Chadha* (1984), it was made clear that the intentions of the parties remain relevant and, even though there is no express mention of this in s.78, that the presumption yields to a contrary intention (there that it was a personal covenant). This means that, where the covenant is not qualified in any way, annexation will readily be inferred: *Crest Nicholson residential South Ltd v McAllister* (2004). If, however, the covenant expressly precludes the benefit from passing then s.78 can have no application. This reflects a sensible interpretation of s.78.

### Express assignment

Express assignment of the covenant (assignment is never implied) is a means of transmitting the benefit to a new purchaser of the dominant land. The assignment must, however, be coupled with a transfer of the land and the conveyance and the assignment must be simultaneous: *Miles v Easter* (1933). It is, therefore, possible for an unbroken chain of assignments to be built up with a new link arising on each sale of the dominant land. There is some force in the argument that, on a post-1925 break in the chain of assignment, s.78 will then operate to statutorily annex the covenant to the land. The difficulty with this "delayed annexation" argument is that, akin to Morrells of *Oxford Ltd v Oxford United FC Ltd* (2001), the original decision to assign might evince a contrary intention to displace the presumption of annexation.

### Scheme of development or building scheme

Such a scheme can operate to pass the benefit of a covenant and will arise where an area of land is developed and the developer subdivides the land into plots and sells those plots to different purchasers. The developer may require each purchaser to enter into a number of covenants to maintain the quality of the estate. Where such a scheme subsists, the purchaser or his assignees can sue and be sued on the mutual obligations. Such a scheme creates a "local law" binding on all owners, irrespective of when the various plots were sold. Equity takes the view that the covenants can be enforced by all owners of land within the scheme. The traditional principles for the existence of a scheme were laid down in *Elliston v Reacher* (1908):

- both parties must derive title under a common vendor;
- the common vendor must have, before selling to either party, laid out the estate, or defined parts thereof, for sale in lots subject to restrictions intended to be imposed on all the lots and which, though varying from lot to lot, are consistent only with a general scheme of development;
- the restrictions were intended by the common vendor to be and were for the benefit of all the lots intended to be sold; and
- the parties to the action, or their predecessors in title purchased their lots from a common vendor on the footing that the restrictions were for the benefit of the other lots in the general scheme.

### Modern relaxation of rules

In more recent times, there has been some retreat from these formal require-ments: *Williams v Kiley* (2003). The courts are now more concerned with the identification of the area to be the subject of the scheme and that the intention was that a scheme of mutually enforceable obligations exist. In *Re Dolphin's Conveyance* (1970), for example, a scheme was held to exist even though there was no common vendor (there were several vendors). Similarly in *Baxter v Four Oaks Properties Ltd* (1965), a scheme was held to exist even though the common vendor had not laid out the estate in lots prior to the sale. Nevertheless, it is necessary that the existence of the scheme must be brought to the knowledge the prospective purchasers: *Emile Elias & Co Ltd v Pine Groves Ltd* (1993).

## TREATING POSITIVE COVENANTS DIFFERENTLY

### The Distinction
Although the benefit of positive freehold covenants can run with the dominant land, it has been long established that the burden of a positive freehold

covenant cannot: *Austerberry v Oldham Corp* (1885). This rule has been criticised by the Law Commission on several occasions. Nevertheless, the rule has subsequently been reaffirmed by the House of Lords in *Rhone v Stephens* (1994). Equity, as Lord Templeman explained, "has no power to enforce positive covenants against successors in title of the land. To enforce such a positive covenant would be to enforce a personal obligation against a person who has not covenanted". Accordingly, equity views a negative covenant as merely depriving an owner of rights that would otherwise have existed. It views positive covenants, however, as being outside the policing of equity because to compel a subsequent owner to comply with such a covenant would contradict the common law rule as to privity of contract. As Lord Templeman continued:

> "Enforcement of a positive covenant lies in contract; a positive covenant compels an owner to exercise his rights. Enforcement of a negative covenant lies in property; a negative covenant deprives the owner of a right over property".

### Sidestepping the rule in Rhone v Stephens

At present, it is possible to circumvent the rule in *Rhone v Stephens* (1994) and this can be achieved in a variety of ways.

*Granting a lease*

Developers might want to sell off plots on a leasehold basis because the burden of both negative and positive leasehold covenants run with the land due to the concept of privity of estate.

*Setting up a commonhold scheme*

Under the **Commonhold and Leasehold Reform Act 2002,** a developer can create a commonhold scheme, say, of a block flats. This is a new type of freehold title which is specifically designed so that the burden of positive covenants can run with the land. It has, however, proved extremely unpopular with developers.

*Chain of indemnity covenants*

If the original covenantor and each successor in title of the servient tenement obtains an indemnity covenant from the next purchaser, the continuing liability of the original covenantor can be offset by a claim of indemnity. This is a cumbersome and unreliable method of passing on responsibility because the system will unravel if there is a break in the chain of indemnities.

## The benefit and burden rule

This prevents a claim to the benefit of a covenant without performing the burden and can be employed to enable the burden of a positive covenant to bind a third party. This is sometimes known as the rule in *Halsall v Brizell* (1957). This means that, if a person wishes to take advantage of a service or facility (e.g. to use a road or drains), he must comply with any consequential obligation that goes with it (e.g. contributing to the maintenance of the road or drains). As in *Shiloh Spinners Ltd v Harding* (1973), this will make the otherwise unenforceable positive covenant enforceable against a new purchaser.

## Case law illustrations

- *Tito v Waddell* (No. 2) (1977), where the successors in title of a mining company who had acquired rights to remove phosphate from the land (the benefit) had to replant the land with indigenous trees and shrubs (perform the burden).
- *Allied London Industrial Properties Ltd v Castleguard Properties Ltd* (1997), where it was argued that, in order to take advantage of a right of way over a road, the purchaser should comply with the positive obligations imposed by a related covenant to carry out road widening. It was held to be outside the benefit and burden rule because the positive covenant was not viewed as a condition of the exercise of the right of way. There was insufficient reciprocity between the right and the covenant.
- *Thamesmead Town Ltd v Allotey* (1998), where the use of a communal space and footpaths was enjoyed by two tenants in the Council overspill estate. The tenants acquired the freehold in their homes and it was claimed that they should make a contribution towards the upkeep of the communal land. The court held that the tenants were free to choose whether to use the rights or not and, if they chose not to, did not have to contribute to the upkeep.

## Enlargement of a long lease into a freehold estate

The resulting fee simple is made subject to all the same covenants and obligations to which the lease is already subject: s.153 of the **LPA**. Positive covenants contained in the lease should, thereby, continue to bind despite of the change to a freehold estate.

## Creating an estate rentcharge

This is made subject to the performance of positive obligations (e.g. to repair or to build). A rentcharge is an annual payment of money charged on the land which can be enforced if the money is not paid. A rentcharge to enforce the performance of positive obligations survives the culling effect of the **Rentcharges Act 1977**.

## DISCHARGE OF RESTRICTIVE COVENANTS

### At Common Law

A restrictive covenant is permanently discharged where the dominant and servient tenements come into common ownership: *Texaco Antilles Ltd v Kernochan* (1973). This rule does not apply to building schemes where the covenant can be revived if the plots later fall once more into separate ownership. Abandonment is a further way in which a covenant may lapse at common law. If abandoned, the covenant will not be enforced: *Chatsworth Estates v Fewell* (1931). This case, however, emphasises the difficulty of proving abandonment.

### Under Statute

A restrictive covenant may be discharged on application to the Lands Tribunal under s.84(1) of the **LPA** (as amended). In making any order, the Lands Tribunal will take into account any development plan and planning policy for the area. Each application is considered on its facts: *University of Westminster v President of the Lands Tribunal* (1998).

#### Grounds

The Lands Tribunal may make a discharge order wherever:

- the restriction is deemed obsolete by virtue of changes in the character of the property or neighbourhood or other material circumstances: *Re Bradley Clare Estates Ltd* (1987);
- the continued existence of the covenant would impede some reasonable user of the land for public or private purposes, and either the covenant confers no practical benefit of substantial value or compensation would be adequate to cover any loss: see *Gilbert v Spoor* (1983);
- the parties entitled to the benefit of the restriction have expressly or impliedly agreed to its discharge or modification. The parties must be of full age and capacity; or
- the proposed discharge or modification will not injure the persons entitled to the benefit of the restriction: see *Moody v Vercan* (1991).

You should now know and understand:

- **The differences between a positive covenant and a negative covenant;**
- the conditions necessary for benefit of a freehold covenant to run at common law;
- the conditions necessary for the benefit and burden of negative freehold covenants to run in equity;
- the ways in which the rule that the burden of positive covenants can never run with the land may be sidestepped.

# QUESTION AND ANSWER

## Question

Heathcliffe was the freeholder of Bronte Farm. In 2002, he sold an adjacent field to Emily. Emily covenanted not to use the field for residential purposes and not to allow a fence, which divided the field from Heathcliffe's farmhouse, to fall into disrepair. Both covenants were expressed to be for the benefit of Bronte Farm. In 2005, Heathcliffe sold Bronte Farm to Jane.

In 2007, Emily sold the field to Old Build Ltd. In December 2009, the fence was severely damaged in a storm. Old Build Ltd has announced plans to build a housing estate on the field and have started to replace the fencing by planting a hedgerow.

On the understanding that any registration requirements have been satisfied, advise Jane.

## Advice and the Answer

This is a straightforward problem question to do with freehold covenants. While Heathcliffe and Emily are the freeholders of the dominant and servient tenements respectively, there is no problem. Heathcliffe (the original covenantee) can enforce the covenants (whether negative or positive) against Emily (the original covenantor). The benefit of the covenant can be assigned by Heathcliffe to a third party by virtue of s.136 of the **Law of Property Act 1925**. There is no suggestion that this has happened on the present facts. Similarly, the benefit can be claimed by a third party under s.56(1) if the covenant makes clear that it is to benefit the non-covenanting party or under s.1 of the **Contracts (Rights of Third Parties) Act 1999** if the other is named or a member of a named class. As both covenants are expressed to benefit the land, with no mention of a third party, be it name or otherwise, these provisions are redundant. Accordingly, when Heathcliffe sells Bronte Farm to Jane it becomes necessary to consider the common law rules as to the running of the benefit of the two freehold covenants. It is important to note that the benefit (but not the burden) of such covenants can run with the dominant land whether the covenant is positive or negative: *Gafford v Graham*. The following conditions set out in *P&A Swift Investments v Combined English Stores Group Plc* must, however, be satisfied. First, the covenant must touch and concern the land (i.e. it must be referable to the land) and not merely be a personal covenant. The covenants relating to the use of the servient land and the fence clearly satisfy this requirement. Secondly, the covenantee (Heathcliffe) must at the time the covenant is given own a freehold estate in the dominant land. This is satisfied on the present facts. Thirdly, the covenant must have been intended to run with the land. On the facts, it is appears that this has been made clear expressly. In any event, and unless there is a contrary intention shown, s.78 of the **Law of Property Act 1925** will imply that intention and deem that the covenants here have been made on behalf of successors in title. There is no contrary intention here and, hence, Jane will most certainly get the benefit of both covenants when she purchases Bronte Farm.

Different considerations apply, however, when Old Build Ltd purchase the servient tenement. It is now necessary to consider whether the burden of the two covenants runs with the servient land and binds the new purchaser. The common law rules are of no relevance now and, instead, the equitable rules concerning the running of the benefit and burden of freehold covenants must be applied. Turning to the burden, only the burden of a negative (i.e. restrictive) covenant can run with the servient land: *Rhone v Stephens*. Accordingly, it is important to consider the nature of the two covenants. The covenant not to use the property for residential purposes is quite clearly negative in both voice and nature. In relation to the covenant not to allow the fence to fall into disrepair, this may at first glance appear negative in nature. It is certainly expressed with a negative voice, but the reality is that it is a positive covenant: *Haywood v Brunswick Permanent Benefit Building Society*. It involves the servient owner in spending energy and money. Accordingly, the burden of this covenant does not transfer to Old Build Ltd and cannot be enforced against the new servient owner. The "user" covenant is the only one, therefore, that can bind Old Build Ltd. In order to ascertain whether this negative covenant does bind, the conditions set out in *Tulk v Moxhay* must be present. As the question states, there is no need to discuss matters of registration. The negative covenant must have been intended to benefit and must touch and concern the dominant land. There appears to be no problem with this as the dominant and servient tenements are adjacent and the dominant tenement clearly identified: *Re Ballard's Conveyance*. It must also be shown that the burden of the covenant was intended to run with the land. This is not done expressly on the present facts. Nevertheless, in the absence of a contrary intention the burden will be deemed to run by virtue of s.79 of the **Law of Property Act 1925**. The "user" covenant will, therefore, bind Old Build Ltd.

It remains to show that Jane has the corresponding benefit of the negative covenant under the equitable rules and not merely at common law. To do this, she must show that there was express or statutory annexation of the benefit to her dominant land. There does not appear to be sufficient here to have express annexation (*Rogers v Hosegood*). Section 78 of the **LPA** may, however, come to the aid of Jane. This provides that a covenant shall be deemed to have been made with the covenantee and successors in title as if the latter had been expressly mentioned: *Federated Homes Ltd v Mill Lodge Properties Ltd*. This gives way to a contrary intention, but no such intention appears on the facts. There is no question of an express assignment of the benefit from Heathcliffe to Jane and no suggestion of a building scheme.

In conclusion, therefore, the fencing covenant cannot be enforced against Old Build Ltd, but the restrictive "user" covenant can be.

# Leasehold Covenants

## 15

## INTRODUCTION

Leasehold covenants lie at the core of the landlord and tenant relationship. They state the formal rights and obligations of the parties under the lease. Covenants can be positive in nature (i.e. they can compel a party to do something, for example, to pay rent and to insure) or they can be negative (i.e. they can restrict a party from doing something, for example, using the premises for business purposes). Both parties usually enter into a series of express covenants (i.e. explicitly stated in the lease) whereas other covenants may be implied by law.

## EXPRESS COVENANTS

The express covenants that may be found in leases are varied and numerous with the tenant tending to give the majority of them. Most commonly, the landlord covenants to give quiet enjoyment and, depending on the type of lease and premises, to keep the property in repair. The tenant usually covenants to pay rent and rates, not to assign without the landlord's consent, to insure and, where the landlord does not so covenant, to repair the property.

### Covenants to Repair
*Meaning*

The meaning of the word "repair" is not clear-cut and the wording of a covenant to repair often varies, e.g. to keep in "good tenantable repair" "substantial repair" or "perfect repair". In *Proudfoot v Hart* (1890), however, these descriptive labels were viewed as merely indicating such repair as, having regard to the age, character and locality of the property, would make it reasonably fit for occupation. The meaning of a covenant is construed as at the time it was granted. Particularly with old buildings, renewal of subsidiary parts might be involved in "repair", but not complete reconstruction: *Brew Bros v Snax* (1970). A covenant which requires the landlord to keep the building in "good and tenantable condition" requires him to put it into that condition: *Credit Suisse v Beegas Nominees Ltd* (1994). A covenant to "keep premises in repair" obliges the covenantor to keep them in repair at all times. A tenant will, therefore, be in breach immediately the defect occurs. A landlord will be in breach only when he knows of the disrepair and has failed to carry out remedial work within a reasonable time: *British Telecommunications v Sun Life Assurance Society* (1995).

### Fair wear and tear

The covenant to repair may contain an exception for "fair wear and tear" which exonerates the covenantor from disrepair arising from the ravages of normal use and normal ageing. However, the covenantor is obliged to take action to prevent fair wear and tear causing other damage to the premises: *Haskell v Marlow* (1928).

### Remedies

The normal remedy for breach of a covenant to repair is damages, although in exceptional cases specific performance may be granted: *Jeune v Queens Cross Properties Ltd* (1974). In terms of damages, the quantum cannot exceed the diminution in the value of the reversion, and no damages can be recovered where the premises are to be demolished or structurally altered so as to make repairs valueless at, or soon after, the end of the term: s.18(1) of the Landlord and Tenant Act 1927. A claim for the cost of alternative accommodation while the premises are uninhabitable is permissible: *Calabar v Stitcher* (1984).

## Covenant against Assigning, Sub-Letting or Parting with Possession
### Meaning

In the absence of any express provision in a lease, a tenant may transfer the property freely by way of assignment, sub-lease or otherwise. Any express provision in the lease will be strictly construed against the tenant: *Marks v Warren* (1979). In *Field v Barkworth* (1986) a covenant not to assign or underlet any part of the premises was broken by an assignment of the whole. In general, a covenant should expressly prohibit assignment, underletting and parting with possession of the whole or any part or parts of the premises.

### Absolute or qualified?

The form of the covenant may be "absolute" or "qualified". Subject to its relaxation by the landlord, an absolute prohibition is enforceable as it stands. A qualified covenant, however, prohibits assignment without the consent of the landlord. Pursuant to s.19(1)(a) of the Landlord and Tenant Act 1927, this consent cannot be unreasonably withheld. A tenant must, however, request consent before he can rely on s.19(1). If consent is withheld, the landlord should notify the tenant in writing and provide reasons: *Footwear Corporation Ltd v Amplight Properties Ltd* (1999).

Section 1(1) of the **Landlord and Tenant Act 1988**, imposes a duty on a landlord to make a decision (once consent is requested under a qualified covenant) within a reasonable time of the tenant's application. If consent has been unreasonably refused, the landlord commits a tort that will entitle the tenant to obtain damages or an injunction.

### Reasonable grounds?

The issue of "reasonableness" was considered in *International Drilling Fluids Ltd v Louisville Investments (Uxbridge) Ltd* (1985). There it was accepted that the landlord could refuse consent only on grounds which had to do with the relationship of landlord and tenant and the subject matter of the lease. The court will proceed in a commonsense manner and decide the issue, on an objective basis, on the facts of a particular case. For example, a landlord might be able reasonably to refuse consent if the proposed assignment would result in a diminution in the rental value of the premises: *Norwich Union Life Assurance Society v Shopmoor Ltd* (1999). As a general rule, it will be unreasonable to withhold consent based upon colour, race, nationality or ethnic or national origins (**Race Relations Act 1976**) or gender (**Sexual Discrimination Act 1975**).

### Advance agreement

Section 22 of the **Landlord and Tenant (Covenants) Act 1995** applies to qualified covenants against assignment of leases of commercial (not residential or agricultural) premises. This provides that a landlord may reasonably withhold consent to any assignment (but not sub-letting or parting with possession) where the circumstances in which he may do so have been set out in an agreement and the circumstances anticipated in the agreement exist. The landlord can, therefore, stipulate in advance the circumstances in which he will refuse consent to the assignment of a tenancy. The landlord may, for example, impose conditions about future guarantees or criteria for assessing the creditworthiness of any proposed assignee. Any veto will automatically be reasonable if within the terms of the agreement.

## IMPLIED OBLIGATIONS

### Landlord's Covenant for Quiet Enjoyment
The tenant has a right to possession at the commencement of the lease and is entitled to damages if his enjoyment is substantially interfered with by acts of

the landlord. Examples of such acts usually take the form of direct physical interference such as disconnecting gas or electricity supplies or disturbance caused by noise or building works: *Southwark LBC v Mills* (2001). Insulting and violent behaviour may also amount to a breach: *Sampson v Floyd* (1989). If a landlord takes all reasonable precautions to avoid disturbance to the tenant when carrying out works, there will be no breach of this covenant: *Goldmile Properties Ltd v Lechouritis* (2003).

## Non-derogatation from Grant

The landlord must not frustrate the use of the land for the purpose for which it was let. For example, if a building is leased for business purposes the landlord cannot do anything which undermines that purpose, for example, blocking the entrance to the tenant's premises: *Owen v Gadd* (1956).

## Repair and Fitness for Habitation

At common law, there is no general guarantee that the premises let are fit for habitation nor is the landlord under an obligation to repair. Nevertheless certain exceptions to this rule exist.

### Furnished dwelling-houses

These must be reasonably fit for human habitation when let: *Smith v Marrable* (1843) (bug-infested premises). Note that this does not extend to unfurnished dwellings.

### Houses let at a low rent

Sections 8–10 of the Landlord and Tenant Act 1985 imply an obligation that the landlord will keep premises fit for human habitation throughout the tenancy.

### Lettings of a dwelling-house for less than seven years

These fall within ss.11–16 of the **Landlord and Tenant Act 1985**. These provisions require the landlord to keep in repair the structure and exterior of the dwelling house, including drains, pipes and gutters. Installations in the house (e.g. for water, gas, electricity, sanitation and heating purposes) must also be kept in repair and proper working order. In *Staves & Staves v Leeds CC* (1991) it was held that dampness in plasterwork was part of the structure and exterior. The landlord was liable despite the fact that the saturation of the plasterwork resulted from an inherent, building defect. A landlord is not, however, liable for inherent defects if their remedy would amount to an improvement to the property.

*Common Parts*

In blocks of flats the landlord usually retains control of the means of access such as lifts and staircases. In these circumstances, the landlord is under a contractual obligation to keep them in repair: *Liverpool Corp v Irwin* (1977).

*Defective premises*

Section 4 of the **Defective Premises Act 1972** requires the landlord to take reasonable care to ensure that persons who might be affected by defects in the premises are reasonably safe from injury or damage. In *Wallace v Manchester CC* (1998) the obligation was breached by a landlord who permitted a collapsed wall, rotten windows, a failed damp proof course, loose plaster and skirting, rat infestation and leaking rainwater pipes.

## Tenant's Implied Obligations

- Not to commit waste. A tenant will usually be liable for "waste" which covers the intentional or negligent deterioration of the property and, accordingly, must keep the premises in repair: *Warren v Kean* (1954).
- To pay rent. The implication is that the rent is payable in arrear and remains payable even if the premises later become unusable by the tenant (e.g. they are damaged by fire).
- To pay rates and taxes in relation to the property. This rule gives way if Parliament imposes a tax to be paid by the landlord.
- To allow the landlord to enter and view the property. This obligation is implied where the landlord has covenanted to repair.

## ENFORCEMENT OF LEASEHOLD COVENANTS

This area of the law has undergone significant change by virtue of the **Landlord and Tenant (Covenants) Act 1995**. The Act became operative on January 1, 1996 and its most significant provisions apply to leases that are created on or after that date. It is necessary, therefore, to know both the old common law rules and the new rules as to enforceability. It will become clear that, for a covenant to be enforced, either privity of contract or privity of estate must exist between the parties.

### Privity of Contract

As between the original parties to the lease, the position is simple: each party can sue the other for breach of covenant. The rule is that this liability continues for the duration of the lease (e.g. until the lease expires, is forfeited or sur-rendered). As it is the tenant who gives the majority of the covenants, original tenant liability is the most striking consequence of this common law rule. It entails that the original tenant can be held to account for breaches of covenant committed by any future assignee years down the line. This is attractive from the landlord's perspective in that he has the option of who to sue: the current tenant (i.e. on the basis of privity of estate) or the original tenant (i.e. on the basis of privity of contract). It is up to the landlord who he wishes to pursue: *Milverton Group Ltd v Warner World Ltd* (1995).

## Continuing liability

The above only applies to who can be sued (i.e. liability), it does not enable the original party to sue once that party has parted with the lease or the rever-sion. Take for example, where the original landlord retains the reversion and the original tenant assigns the lease to the assignee. The landlord subsequently is in breach of his repair covenant. Only the assignee can make a claim against the landlord. The original tenant cannot pursue an action after parting with the lease. If it were otherwise it would mean that the landlord could be sued by two characters (the current tenant and the original tenant) for the same breach and, therefore, might have to pay double compensation. As the original tenant has suffered no loss, it would be unjust to expose the original landlord to this type of additional liability. As regards pre-assignment breaches, however, the former tenant can still sue for loss that occurred while he was a tenant even though the lease has since been assigned: *City & Metropolitan Properties v Greycroft* (1987).

### And sub-tenants

The creation of a sub-tenancy by the tenant entails that the tenant remains liable for breaches of covenant in the main lease even though the fault may lie with the sub-tenant. There is no direct relationship of privity of contract or estate between a head landlord and a sub-tenant so that as a general rule neither can sue the other directly.

### Assigning the reversion

Assignment by the original landlord preserves the original landlord's liability to the original tenant for breaches committed by his assignee. It is to be noted that:

- the original tenant has an option of suing the original landlord (privity of contract) or the current landlord (privity of estate: see below);

- the right to sue the original tenant for pre-assignment breaches of covenant passes automatically to the new landlord under s.141 of the **LPA** without the need for an express transfer of the benefit of the contract. For this purpose alone, privity of contract exists between the new landlord and the original tenant: *London and County (A & D) Ltd v Wilfred Sportsman Ltd* (1971);
- the original landlord cannot sue the original tenant once the reversion has been assigned.

## Privity of Estate
### Meaning

In order to make the leasehold system work, the covenants have to be made binding on third parties (i.e. the assignees of the landlord and tenant). This is achieved by a concept known as "privity of estate". It entails that the covenants become imprinted on the estate and are always enforceable by and against the current landlord and the current tenant: *City of London Corporation v Fell* (1994). This is necessary as the contractual relationship exists only between the original parties and they may die or become insolvent many years before the end of the lease. Privity of estate exists independently from, and parallel to, the contract which created the covenant. If an original tenant is released from liability, this leaves unaffected the liability of the current tenant. An assignee is only liable whilst he holds the lease or reversion and after that time there is no longer any privity of estate between the parties.

### Touching and concerning

Assignees are only bound by covenants which "touch and concern the land" (i.e. a covenant that is referable to the land and not merely personal: ss.141 and 142 of the **LPA 1925**). This is known as the rule in Spencer's case (1583). Covenants by the tenant to pay rent or repair would "touch and concern" the land, but a covenant to pay rates on other land would not. A covenant by the landlord to renew the lease would "touch and concern", but not a covenant to sell the reversion at a stated price at the tenant's option. A covenant does not "touch and concern" merely because its breach may cause forfeiture of the lease.

### Working illustrations

- L grants a lease to T for 20 years. For the duration of the lease, L and T are in privity of contract with one another which means that they can sue each other for breaches of covenant.

- T assigns the lease to A. As privity of contract still exists between L and T, L can sue T, but T can no longer sue L. As privity of estate now exists between L and A, A can sue L directly (and vice versa) on those covenants which "touch and concern" the land.
- L then assigns the reversion to R, privity of estate now exists between R and A. There is neither privity of estate nor privity of contract between R and T. Consequently only A and R can sue each other on any covenant which relates to the land.
- If A grants a subtenancy to S and S is in breach of a covenant in the headlease (the lease between L & T), there is no privity of estate nor contract between R and S. R cannot sue S directly. R will have to sue A and A will hope to pass liability on to S.

## Indemnity

In the light of the original landlord/tenant remaining liable for breaches of covenant by a future assignee, it is understandable that the original party can, in certain circumstances, claim indemnity from the true wrongdoer.

### Indemnity covenants

In every assignment of the tenancy (but not the reversion) there is implied an indemnity covenant (s.77 of the **LPA 1925**) which entitles the original tenant to sue the assignee next in the chain, but no other assignee. This assignee will then pass responsibility down the chain and this process will continue until, hopefully, responsibility reaches the assignee at fault. Where there is a break in the chain (e.g. a former assignee is now dead) financial responsibility arbitrarily stops at the assignee next before the break. As regards assignments of the landlord's reversion there is no implied covenant and an express covenant should be taken on each assignment. This is also so when a sub-tenancy is created at which time the sub-tenant should give his immediate landlord an express indemnity covenant.

**Figure 16: Indemnity Covenants**

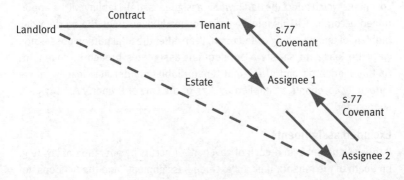

*Moule v Garrett*

At common law, there exists a rule of common honesty which means that if, say, a tenant is under legal compulsion to pay an assignee's debt, the tenant can recover the money directly from the assignee in default: *Moule v Garrett* (1872).

## The Landlord and Tenant (Covenants) Act 1995
*Background*

The major criticism of the common law was the continuing liability of the original tenant throughout the lease and the potential liability of such tenants for breaches of covenant committed after an assignment of the lease had taken place. These injustices have, however, been tackled by the **Landlord and Tenant (Covenants) Act 1995**. The Act makes fundamental changes to the law affecting continuing liability both of tenants and landlords. The primary focus of the Act is to relieve the parties from ongoing liability. This aspect of the Act applies only to tenancies created on or after January 1, 1996. Indeed, most of the provisions are prospective only, i.e. they apply only tenancies which are granted after the date the Act came into force. These are ss.3–16 and s.21. For example, the provisions regarding the transmission and release of covenants; the apportionment of liability between assignor and assignee; the abolition of statutory indemnity covenants; and the former tenant's guarantee of assignee's performance of covenants. Some apply to both old and new tenancies: ss.17–20. These concern default notices served on former tenants and guarantors; the consequences of variation of leasehold terms; and the right to an overriding lease.

## Abolition of original tenant liability
The real sea change is to be found in s.5. Under this provision the tenant is *automatically* released from original tenant's liability on the lawful assignment of the *whole* of the premises demised. This reflects a "clean break" idea. If *part* only of the premises is assigned, the release applies only as regards the covenants which affect the part lawfully assigned: s.5(3). Liability will be apportioned accordingly. This release scheme clearly overcomes the modern day problem of tenants being called upon, years after the total parting possession with the lease, to satisfy a subsequent assignee's breach of covenant. As this marks the end of original tenant liability under new leases, those indemnity covenants as implied by s.77 of the **Law of Property Act 1925** are superseded.

## Excluded assignments
If the assignment is in breach of covenant or occurs by operation of law (e.g. on death of the tenant), it is an "excluded assignment" and the Act does not

apply to that transaction (s.11). The primary aims are to prevent the original tenant's estate benefiting from an involuntary assignment and to avoid the tenant from escaping liability (and depriving the landlord of the opportunity to take a guarantor) by a prohibited assignment. The assignee will, in these circumstances, also be bound by the leasehold covenants. The provisions of the 1995 Act will bite, however, on the next assignment of the lease or reversion which is not excluded.

## Authorised Guarantee Agreement

As regards new leases, and although released from liability, the tenant may still be required by the landlord to enter "an authorised guarantee" agreement ("AGA") with respect to the performance of the leasehold covenants by the assignee. The assignor will, thereby, be liable for the performance of covenants by his assignee, but no other (s.16). As the original tenant would now be a guarantor, the release of the assignee from liability (e.g. by agreement or on insolvency) will also release the assignor/guarantor. On a future assignment, the next assignor will give a new AGA to the landlord.

## Original landlord liability

The Act also offers protection for the landlord who assigns the reversion. Section 6 allows the lessor (and any former landlord) to be released from the original covenants following the lawful assignment of the reversion of the *whole* premises. This is not, however, automatic and, in default of agreement, can only follow a s.8 application. This qualified right reflects the reality that the landlord has more effective remedies than the tenant for breach of covenant (e.g. forfeiture) and, consequently, does not need the same degree of protection. If release is refused the former landlord can re-apply on the next assignment of the reversion. If *part* of the reversion is lawfully assigned, the landlord (or former landlord) can apply for release of the covenants which affect that part.

## Section 8 procedure

A written notice following a prescribed form must be served by the landlord either before or within four weeks after the assignment of the reversion. This notice must inform the tenant that the assignment is to take place or, as appropriate, has taken place. The notice must contain the request that the covenant(s) as specified are to be released. By virtue of s.8(2), the landlord's application will be successful if either the tenant does not, within four weeks of the landlord's notice, serve a written notice of objection on the landlord (as occurred in *Chesterfield Properties v BHP Petroleum* (2001)); does serve such notice, but the county court decides that it is reasonable for the landlord to be released; or the tenant in writing withdraws any earlier objection. The landlord's release is backdated to the time of assignment.

## Sub-tenants

Although the position of sub-tenants is unaffected by the 1995 Act, in relation to "user covenants", s.3(5) allows such a covenant to be enforceable not only against the assignee, but also against any person (e.g. sub-tenant) who is the owner or occupier of the premises. This applies only to new leases. It facilitates direct enforcement by the landlord against the person who is using the premises in a manner prohibited by the lease.

## Contracting out

Section 25 prohibits contracting out of the Act. The Act was intended to offer an escape route for the tenant and (to a lesser extent) the landlord. Accordingly, the parties can agree to enlarge the escape route by contractual variation, but cannot narrow it. In *London Diocesan Fund v Avonridge Property Co Ltd* (2005), the tenant held under a lease of a number of shop units. The tenant granted subleases of the shops. The tenant subsequently assigned the leases to a third party who fell into rent arrears. The sub-tenant was granted relief against forfeiture on the basis that he paid the outstanding rent. The sub-tenant then sued the tenant under a covenant contained in the subleases that the tenant would pay the rent in the head lease. The covenant, however, specified that the tenant's liability would cease once the tenant parted with the leases. The sub-tenant argued that this restriction was void due to s.25 (i.e. it amounted to unlawful contracting out of the 1995 Act). By a majority, the House of Lords held that the 1995 Act was designed to provide an exit route for the landlord and tenant from ongoing liability. It did not prohibit an agreement that the parties' liability was to be curtailed at the outset or subsequently.

## Personal covenants

The 1995 Act applies to both landlord and tenant covenants whether or not they touch and concern the land and whether the covenant is express, implied or imposed by law: ss.2–3. The general rule now is that the benefit and burden of all (except personal covenants) will run. Personal obligations will not, therefore, be released on an assignment. In *Chesterfield Properties v BHP Petroleum* (2001) certain repair covenants given by the landlord, Chesterfield, were expressed to be of a "personal" nature. The issue which arose was whether these remained "landlord's covenants" governed by the 1995 Act. The landlord subsequently assigned the reversion. Nevertheless, the tenant later claimed against Chesterfield for loss arising from disrepair. It was held by the Court of Appeal that the Act did not release the landlord from personal covenants. This did not offend the contracting out prohibition contained in s.25. They were not "landlord covenants" for these purposes. The landlord was still bound after assignment of the reversion.

## Overriding leases

As regards both *old* and *new* tenancies, the Act gives the tenant or guarantor who discharges, in full, the liability of the assignee, the right to have the landlord grant an overriding lease of the premises demised (s.19). This overriding lease will normally be granted for a term equal to the remainder of the original lease plus three days. The overriding lease will, essentially, be on the same terms as the original. The motivation for taking such an interposed lease could be to allow the tenant to forfeit the assignee's lease and so re-use or reassign (at a premium or market rent) the premises. A claim to exercise the right to an over-riding lease is made by the claimant making a written request to the landlord, within 12 months of the payment, specifying the qualifying payment made. Following such request, the landlord must grant the overriding lease within a reasonable time.

## Fixed charges

Whether under an old or a new tenancy, where the original tenant remains liable beyond assignment (including under an "authorised guarantee agreement"), there are imposed restrictions on the recovery of rent or service charges (s.17). There is, in short, a need for six months advance notification of liability for fixed sums by the service of a default notice. The original tenant (and guarantor) will only be liable for rent or service charge (or liquidated damages) if served, within six months of the money becoming "due", with a landlord's notice detailing the default (see *Scottish & Newcastle Plc v Raguz* (2009)). The notice fixes the amount in question and the tenant or guarantor is under no obligation to pay anything more unless:

- liability is subsequently determined to be for a greater amount;
- the notice informed the tenant/guarantor of such a possibility; and,
- the landlord had within three months of the determination served a further notice detailing the greater amount.

## Variation of terms

As regards a new tenancy where there exists an authorised guarantee agreement, or in the case of an old tenancy where original tenant's liability persists, the guarantor or original tenant will not be bound by a variation of the terms occurring after assignment (s.18). This is designed to impose a maximum ceiling on the potential liability ensuring that the guarantor/original tenant will not be liable to pay any excess attributable to that variation of terms. This does not apply to variations in rent following the rent review machinery in the original lease.

You should now know and understand:

- the types of express and implied covenants that might be encountered;

- the concept of privity of contract and the problem of original tenant liability;

- the concept of privity of estate;

- the changes introduced by the **Landlord and Tenant (Covenants) Act 1995.**

## QUESTION AND ANSWER

### Question

(a) In 1994, K (the fee simple owner of a large agricultural estate) leased Larchwood Manor, by deed to L for 21 years at a rent of £25,000 per annum. The lease contained a covenant by K to keep Larchwood Manor in repair. L validly assigned the lease to M in 2002 and M validly assigned the lease to N in 2008. K has recently allowed Larchwood Manor to fall into disrepair. N has not paid the annual rent.

Advise the parties.

### Advice and the Answer

This question relates to the rules governing the enforceability of covenants between parties to a lease and their assignees. Significant changes to this area of law have been made by the **Landlord and Tenant (Covenants) Act 1995** which became operative on January 1, 1996. Given that the present lease was granted in 1994 the old common law rules will govern enforceability.

The relationship between K and L is one of *privity of contract* in that they are the original landlord and tenant. The effect of this is that both K & L remain liable on their covenants for the whole term of the lease, notwithstanding any assignment of the lease or the reversion: *Warnford Investments Ltd v Duckworth*. On the assignment of the lease to M, this creates a relationship of *privity of estate* between K and M which lasts only for the duration of the period that M holds the lease. The consequence of privity of estate is that the benefit and burden will pass of all covenants that "touch and concern" the land (*Spencer's* case). Covenants to repair property and to pay rent clearly touch and concern the land.

As between K and N there is privity of estate, they being the current landlord and the current tenant, respectively. In relation to the breach of K's covenant to repair, this means that N can sue K for breach of covenant. As L has assigned the lease and, hence, suffered no loss he cannot bring an action in contract against his former landlord. Similarly, the intervening assignee (M) is unable to bring an action.

Privity of contract and estate do, however, give K a dual possibility in terms of his ability to sue. He can attempt to recover the rent arrears from L in privity of contract or sue N directly under privity of estate. Although L and N may both therefore be responsible for breach of the covenants, K can only obtain satisfaction from one: *City of London Corporation v Fell*. In respect of the liability of L and N, primary liability is on the person causing the breach, namely N. If K chooses to sue L in *privity of contract* (a course which may be motivated by the respective financial status of N) the issue arises as to whether L can recover any damages he has to pay to K. It is usual for an assignor to take a covenant of indemnity from the assignee, thereby guarding against future breaches of covenant. L may have taken such an indemnity from M. In the absence of any express indemnity, s.77(1)(c) of the LPA 1925 implies an indemnity in any assignment for value, which may be the case here. This will allow L to pass on liability to M. M will then seek to pass on this liability to N under their indemnity covenant. By way of an alternative, L can claim indemnity directly from N under the rule in *Moule v Garrett*. This enables a joint debtor, who has paid money to a common creditor for the exclusive benefit of the other co-debtor, to recover direct from that person. Consequently if L pays damages to K in respect of any breach for which N is responsible then by application of this principle L can recover direct from N and need not sue through the chain involving M.

# Handy Hints

## 16

## Examination tips

Land law is a case law and statute law subject. You have to memorise case names (even if only partially) and statutory provisions and apply them to support your arguments and assertions.

Always attempt the required number of questions on an examination paper. Try to spread your time evenly and remember more marks may be gained at the beginning of a new question than when finishing off an existing question.

Look at past papers and familiarise yourself with the types of questions that are set.

Practise hand writing essay and problem style questions (within exam type conditions) and ask your tutor to look over them. Write as clearly as you can and underline the case names that you use so that they stand out.

Make sure that you revise sensibly and comprehensively. If you cut your revision down to the bare minimum, you may live to regret it. Remember a topic might not appear at all on the paper or might appear in a form that you find difficult.

Try to keep calm both during the revision period and the examination itself.

# Index

This index has been prepared using Sweet and Maxwell's Legal Taxonomy. Main index entries conform to keywords provided by the Legal Taxonomy except where references to specific documents or non-standard terms (denoted by quotation marks) have been included. These keywords provide a means of identifying similar concepts in other Sweet & Maxwell publications and online services to which keywords from the Legal Taxonomy have been applied. Readers may find some minor differences between terms used in the text and those which appear in the index.

Suggestions to **sweetandmaxwell.taxonomy@thomson.com**.